Confessions of a HOT MESS- from MESS to MESSage

90 Days of MESSages for the Hot Mess in You

Leslie Speas

KW
KingdomWinds
PUBLISHING

Copyright © 2021 by Leslie Speas

All rights reserved. No part of this publication may be reproduced, distributed, or transmitted in any form or by any means, including photocopying, recording, or other electronic or mechanical methods, without the prior written permission of the publisher, except in the case of brief quotations embodied in critical reviews and certain other noncommercial uses permitted by copyright law. For permission requests, write to the publisher at publishing@kingdomwinds.com.

Unless otherwise indicated, all Scripture references are taken from the Holy Bible, New International Version®, NIV® Copyright © 1973, 1978, 1984, 2011 by Biblica, Inc.® Used by permission. All rights reserved worldwide.

First Edition, 2021

ISBN 10: 978-1-64590-027-6

Published by Kingdom Winds Publishing.

www.kingdomwinds.com

publishing@kingdomwinds.com

Printed in the United States of America.

Table of Contents

Introduction: Something New! — 7

Section 1: Understanding and Caring for Yourself

Who Am I? — 11
Why Am I Here? — 14
Caring for Your Soul — 17
Caring for Your Body — 20
Making Change Happen — 23
Loving Yourself — 26
Be with Someone Good for Your Soul — 29
Say No to Emotional Abuse — 31
Breaking Through Our Busy — 34
Self-Care is Not Selfish — 37

Section 2: Loving and Caring for Others

Love Your Neighbor as Yourself — 43
Love Your Enemies - Wait, What? — 46
Be Quick to Listen and Slow to Speak — 49
More on Listening — 52
Find Yourself by Serving Others — 54
Who Are We to Judge? — 56
Build 'Em Up — 59
Constructive Criticism — 62
Compassionate Conflict — 64
We All Bleed the Same — 67
Blinded by Our Biases — 70
Leading with Love — 72
Are You Trustworthy? — 74
Impeccable Integrity — 77
RESPECT — 80

Section 3: Managing Your Mind

Taming My Crazy Mind — 85
I Am Enough! — 87
Comparison - The Thief of Joy — 90
Do Not Conform to the Standards of This World — 93
Grace Not Works — 96
Let Go and Let God — 98
Facing Your Fears — 100

Attacking Anxiety	103
Worry Woman	105
Stress Less	107
Anger Management	109
Marvelous Mindfulness	111
Growth as a Mindset	114
Overthink Much?	116
What's Trust Got to Do with It?	118
Guilt Be Gone!	121
Jesus Take the Wheel	124

Section 4: Hot Mess Issues

I Am a Recovering People-Pleaser	129
Perfectly Imperfect	132
Managing My Image	134
The Secret to Parenting	136
It's Hard to Be Humble	140
Pompously Prideful	143
American Idol	146
I Deserve More!	148
Praying Out Loud Challenged	150
When You Doubt…	153
The Waiting Is the Hardest Part	156
I Can't Get No Satisfaction	160
A Simpler Life	163
Don't Be a Debbie Downer	165
Battling Body Image	168
Mirror, Mirror on the Wall	171
Wrinkles and Blemishes	173
Proverbs 31 Woman vs. Hot Mess	175
Abnormal Is Better Than Normal	178

Section 5: SOS (Strength Out of Struggles)

Avoiding Temptation	183
Practicing Self-Control	186
Rejecting Rejection	189
Define or Refine?	192
Pruning My Spiritual Garden	195
Spiritual Warrior	197
When Things Don't Go as Planned	200
Disheartening Discouragement	203

Making Insecurity Insignificant 206
Liberation from Loneliness 209
Turning a Setback into a Comeback! 212
GRIEF- Grace Results in Enduring Hope for Us ... 215

Section 6: Everything Else

Get Out of Jail Free Card 219
Fearless Faith 221
Heavenly Hope 223
Joy to the World 225
Laughter Is the Best Medicine 227
He Is with Me Always 229
How Do You Want to Be Remembered? 231
Christians Can Have Fun Too! 233
What Should I Do in My Quiet Time? 236
Divine Discernment 239
Down with the Drama! 242
Surviving Organizational Politics 245
Bypassing Bullying 247
Being a Team Player 249
Victory Over Victim Mentality 252
Don't Be a "Church Lady" 254
Issues, Issues, and More Issues 256

Section 7: Bonus Chapters

Dear Younger Me 260
Why Can't People Be More Like Dogs? 263
In Conclusion 267
Sources 269

Leslie Speas

Introduction: Something New!

> *"For I am about to do something new. See, I have already begun! Do you not see it? I will make a pathway through the wilderness. I will create rivers in a dry wasteland"* (Isaiah 43:19 NLT).

Have you ever felt called to do something? I used to worry that God might call me to be a missionary in a third-world country—without running water, electricity, or Starbucks. He hasn't called me to do that, but I've had a strong conviction for the last few years that he wants me to share my struggles through writing with the hope that it will help others. Who knew that putting myself out there and sharing what a hot mess I am would be my calling? And who am I to write a Christian book? I think I'm a decent writer, but I haven't been to seminary or had any related formal education. However, I've felt a continued nudge that hasn't wavered that this is what He wants me to do. So, I started a blog and now have written a book.

In *Holy Ambition*, Chip Ingram talks about the people God uses:

> God has chosen very regular, ordinary, common people just like you and me to accomplish the biggest events in all of human history. He used a teenage girl to bring His Son into this planet. He used a blue-collar worker to raise Him from childhood and teach Him about a life of integrity and worship. He used common fishermen to lay the foundation for the greatest revolution that has ever touched the world. And God wants to use you and God wants to use me in the same ways.

> *"For consider your calling, brothers: not many of you were wise according to worldly standards, not many were powerful, not many were of noble birth. But God chose what is foolish in the world to shame the wise; God chose what is weak in the world to shame the strong..."* (1 Corinthian 1:26-27 ESV).

He even uses hot messes like me! What is a hot mess? Here are a few definitions:

- When someone's thoughts or appearance are in a state of disarray, but they maintain an undeniable attractiveness or beauty (urban dictionary)

- A person or thing that is spectacularly unsuccessful or disordered, especially one that is a source of peculiar fascination (dictionary.com)

Here are some hot mess examples for you. Just yesterday, I was to speak at an event for a local organization during lunch. I walked the dogs before I left for work and forgot to change from my tennis shoes. Also, it rained most of the day, and I forgot my umbrella, so, by lunchtime, my curly hair looked like an alpaca. And what's the difference between a llama and an alpaca? See, this is how my brain works. Today I turned on the blender to make my morning smoothie and forgot to put the lid on.

I have lots of other examples that you'll see in this book. I compare. I have a crazy brain. I people-please. I try to control. I can't cook, or keep plants alive, or do arts and crafts.

I generally look fairly put together, but the rest of me often isn't. So, I think we have now established that I'm a hot mess and that God chooses ordinary, foolish people. Let's move back to the "new thing" I'm doing. Sometimes we stay mired in the "as is" and don't trust Him to move forward with the new thing. Although it has taken me way out of my comfort zone, I'm glad that I'm doing the new thing and can't wait to see what the next new thing will be.

If you aren't sure of your calling, ask God to give you eyes to see, ears to hear, and a heart to do His will, and He will lead you towards your purpose.

"For we are God's masterpiece. He has created us anew in Christ Jesus, so we can do the good things he planned for us long ago" (Ephesians 2:10 NLT).

Section 1:

Understanding and Caring for Yourself

LESLIE SPEAS

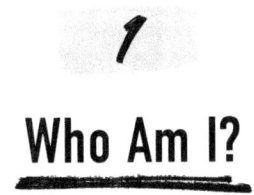

Who Am I?

Humans are definitely a complicated mix of experiences, thoughts, and emotions. Many people go through life not really understanding themselves, what motivates them, and why they do what they do. I believe that it's important for us to take time to know ourselves in order to maximize our potential.

It has taken me years to understand myself better, and I have just recently come to know who I am in Christ. For a long time, there were things from my past that I let guide my thoughts, emotions, and behavior, and I didn't realize that this was even happening. I guess I just kind of operated on autopilot. Shame and rejection from previous experiences in my life were affecting me. I was also operating from a narrative that I wasn't good enough.

I believe that the journey of self-discovery begins with knowing and understanding Jesus. For a truthful look at who we are, we must look into the Bible as we are told to use God's Word as a mirror to truly understand ourselves. James 1:22-24 says, *"Do not merely listen to the word, and so deceive yourselves. Do what it says. Anyone who listens to the word but does not do what it says is like a man who looks at his face in a mirror and, after looking at himself, goes away and immediately forgets what he looks like."*

God tells us to examine ourselves and our actions. (1 Corinthians 11:28; 2 Corinthians 13:5; Galatians 6:4) When we look at ourselves using His Word, we can see where we are, how we can improve, and where repentance is needed.

Knowing ourselves involves a strong awareness of our personalities, including our struggles, strengths and weaknesses, thoughts and beliefs, motivations, and emotions. It took some time, self-reflection, and counseling for me to better understand myself and what was driving me. Although some Christians hesitate to go to counseling, I truly believe that almost everyone can benefit from it. Sometimes we need an outside person to help facilitate understanding of ourselves. Although self-reflection and counseling have been helpful, the thing that has most impacted my journey towards self-discovery is my faith and my deepening relationship with Jesus.

Jesus was the most self-aware person ever. He knew who he was, why he was on earth, and what he needed to do to accomplish his mission. Peter is an example of someone who wasn't so self-aware. At the Last Supper, Jesus predicted that Peter would deny him. Peter adamantly pledged that he wouldn't, but then he denied Jesus three times before the rooster crowed. When he realized what he had done, he cried bitterly (Matthew 26).

Self-discovery can be difficult and painful because it involves dredging up unpleasant things from our past. However, we need to do this to move to higher ground. Here are a few ideas that might be helpful in getting to know yourself better:

Take an assessment

Some common assessments are the Enneagram, Myers Briggs Type Indicator, DISC, StrengthsFinder, and there are several Spiritual Gifts Inventories. At work, we use an assessment which helps you understand how you are wired. I am a Merchant/Builder, which means I'm a relationship-builder who is action-oriented. This has pretty much been the underlying theme in my assessments over the years. I also know that I am pretty much right in the middle of introvert and extrovert, which helps me to better understand why I need some alone time to recharge most days since I generally have to "extrovert" at work.

Explore what guides and motivates you

Ask yourself questions like:
- Who am I really?
- Why am I here?
- What inspires me?
- What makes me unique?
- What do I do well?
- What don't I do well?
- Where am I going?

Ask others for feedback

Ask other people who are close to you questions like:
- What behaviors are limiting my potential?
- What do you think are my strengths and weaknesses?
- How would you describe me to others?
- Is there anything you avoid saying to me because you're afraid of my reaction?

Ask God for help

Spend time with God and ask Him to help you in your quest to better understand yourself. *"Search me, O God, and know my heart; test me and know my anxious thoughts. Point out anything in me that offends you, and lead me along the path of everlasting life" (Psalm 139:23-24 NLT).*

Confessions of a Hot Mess - from MESS to MESSage

The Bible says we should *"put off your old self...and to put on the new self, created after the likeness of God in true righteousness and holiness" (Colossians 3:9-10 ESV)*. When you discover your faults, temptations, blind spots, and negative thought patterns, pray through them and ask God to help you move past these things so that you can grow into your full potential and be who He created you to be.

REFLECT

- Spend some time reflecting on who you are using the suggestions in this lesson.

_____
_____
_____
_____
_____
_____
_____
_____
_____
_____
_____
_____
_____
_____
_____
_____
_____
_____
_____
_____
_____
_____
_____

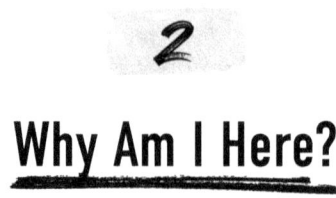

Why Am I Here?

Have you ever wondered about your purpose or calling in life? I know I have, and it's taken me fifty-plus years for it to become clear. I have learned that it is in Christ that we find out who we are and what we are living for. Before we were ever formed, he had his eye and his designs on us for glorious living, as part of the overall purpose he is working out in everything and everyone. We all have our own unique calling, which is where our passion, gifts, and talents, and the world's deepest needs intersect. Jeremiah 1:5 says, *"Before I formed you in the womb I knew you, before you were born I set you apart; I appointed you as a prophet to the nations."* This tells us that God knew what our calling would be and how we were meant to impact the world before we were even conceived.

I grew up, finished college, and began working. Soon to follow was marriage, kids, divorce, marriage again with a blended family, and career through all of that. I didn't come up for air for about twenty years or take the time to specifically articulate a calling. I generally was aware of what I was good at and what I wasn't. Cooking, or really any domestic tasks, were definitely not in my area of talent. In fact, I remember my daughters asking one night what we were having for dinner, and they cheered when I told them frozen dinners. My stepdaughter said that pinto beans (from a can) were my best dish. And my neighbor texts me every time he hears a fire truck nearby to see if I'm cooking. Crafts are not a strength for me either. We did a rotation for leading the elementary kids' Sunday School class years ago. On my rotation, we made popsicle stick crosses and drew designs on them. Very creative, right? So, we have established some of the things I don't do well.

I am pretty adept at communication, building relationships, project management, and leading teams. I probably naturally used my gifts and talents in my job and, to an extent, in the world. However, I had never really articulated my calling or made a concerted effort to work towards a particular purpose. It often felt like I was just trying to get through the day.

When my kids got older and I eventually became an empty nester (ish - they keep coming back), I became more introspective and wanted more clarity on why I'm here on this earth and what I should focus on for the rest of my life. I attended a leadership training class where we went through some activities to articulate our calling. Mine sounds much like the YMCA mission statement. It is "to help others to reach their God-given potential." I feel I have done some of this in my roles in the Human Resources field and, of course, tried to help my children in this way. However, having my calling articulated has made a big difference for me. I have been using it as a filter in prioritizing my life and activities.

If you aren't sure what your calling is, here are some tips to help you discover it.

Listen to your life

Start by answering these questions:
- If money were not an issue, what would you do with your time?
- What do you love to do?
- What gives you energy?
- What drains the life out of you?
- What do you want to change, shape, and leave better than you found it?
- What segment of the population are you drawn to help?
- What are your gifts and talents? It is also helpful to ask others this question to get an outside perspective.

Write your calling

Keep it simple and general enough that you don't pigeonhole yourself. Remember that it can be a changing, living document.

Dream

Let ideas flow on ways you can use your passion. Narrow your list to two or three. Submit these ideas to God and wait for him for confirmation.

Put your passion into action

Devise a plan to put your calling into action in your personal and professional life. Identify any of the cages that limit you (fear, insecurity, perfectionism, etc.) and try to get past these to step into your God-given adventure. Pray about ways you can use your calling, and let the spirit guide you.

Consider the Scriptures below as they relate to your unique calling.

- "For just as each of us has one body with many members, and these members do not all have the same function..." (Romans 12:4).

- *"And we know that in all things God works for the good of those who love him, who have been called according to his purpose"* (Romans 8:28).

REFLECT

- If you aren't sure of your calling, go through the steps above to articulate it, and develop an action plan to bring it to life!

3

Caring for Your Soul

"What good is it for someone to gain the whole world, yet forfeit their soul?" (Matthew 8:36).

In my women's Bible study group, we had a discussion about the soul. I asked if anyone could define "soul," and no one seemed to have a good definition. One of my friends said that it's like a little person inside you. This cracked me up. It reminded me of the little devil and angel on each shoulder trying to influence someone's actions that I have seen on various shows/movies.

This conversation led me to do some research on the soul. Here are a few definitions that I liked:

- the part of a person that is not physical and lasts eternally as a person experiences death

- the fabric that represents us, our entire element of existence

First Thessalonians 5:23 says that we are all created with a spirit, soul, and body: *"May God himself, the God of peace, sanctify you through and through. May your whole spirit, soul and body be kept blameless at the coming of our Lord Jesus Christ."*

The body is obviously our outermost and visible part, and by it, we exist and experience things in the physical world. Our soul, though unseen, is just as real. It is made up of our mind, emotions, and will and is essentially who we are within. The spirit is the deepest and hidden part of our being. Through our spirit, we can contact the spiritual realm and be in continuous contact with God.

In our world, we exert most of our energy satisfying the body's appetites and almost none to the soul, which requires just as much, if not more, attention. When we feel empty, overwhelmed, or alienated, we tend to drown our thirst for God with distractions like television, social media, the internet, shopping, and work instead of being silent and listening to our souls' needs. Nothing but God ever completely satisfies us because the soul was made for Him and, without him, is restless.

In Psalm 42:1,5, David says, *"As the deer pants for streams of water, so my soul pants for you, O God....Why are you downcast, O my soul? Why so disturbed within me? Put your hope in God, for I will yet praise him, my Savior and my God."*

I'm at a place in my life where I have more time to spend caring for my soul. I remember how challenging it was to have small children and a full-time job. It was difficult to have any time to focus on myself. However, it's important to make time when you can, even if it's just ten or fifteen minutes a day. If you don't provide your soul with the rest and recharge it needs, your well will run dry, and you won't have any energy to pour out to others.

What can you do to feed your soul? Here are some things that help me:
- Practicing quiet time with God in the morning or whenever I can fit it in
- Reading
- Spending time in nature
- Yoga
- Exercising
- Laughing
- Helping or serving others
- Cuddling my dogs

Sometimes you have to let things go to take care of your soul. Over the past ten years, I have let go of two jobs that negatively impacted my well-being. Both of these jobs involved chaotic environments and leadership styles that weren't good for my soul. In addition, you may have to let go of relationships that are draining your energy. I have had to let go of several friendships over the years that were emotionally draining.

Finally, to take good care of your soul, you will have to release some of the other things that we will cover in this book–comparison, negative thought patterns, control, and people-pleasing -to name a few!

Take some time to care for your soul! What could be more important?

REFLECT

- What gets in the way of caring for your soul?
- What actions could you take to feed your soul?
- What could you eliminate from your life to focus more on caring for your soul?

Confessions of a Hot Mess - from MESS to MESSage

Caring for Your Body

"Do you not know that your body is a temple of the Holy Spirit, who is in you, whom you have received from God? You are not your own; you were bought at a price. Therefore honor God with your body" (1 Corinthians 6:19-20).

Your body is the vessel that carries your soul and spirit while you are on this earth. We have established that it's important to nurture our souls. But we can do what we want with our bodies, right? Not so much. To care for your soul and spirit, you must also care for your body.

You live your entire life in your body—the one and only body God created for you in which to do his will and work. Unfortunately, we often mistreat this body, and we don't realize that it affects how well we can live out our God-given purpose. Said differently, we need to have a healthy vessel to best serve the Lord.

First Corinthians has a lot to say about our bodies:

- *"Don't you know that you yourselves are God's temple and that God's spirit dwells in your midst? If anyone destroys God's temple, God will destroy that person; for God's temple is sacred and you together are that temple" (1 Corinthians 3:16-17).*

- *"So whether you eat or drink or whatever you do, do it all for the glory of God" (1 Corinthians 10:31).*

- *"Do you not know that your body is a temple of the Holy Spirit, who is in you, whom you have received from God? You are not your own; you were bought at a price. Therefore honor God with your body" (1 Corinthians 6:19-20).*

Our bodies are part of our service and worship to God, and we honor Him by taking care of our "temples." Romans 12:1 says, *"Therefore, I urge you brothers and sisters, in view of God's mercy, to offer your bodies as living sacrifices, holy and pleasing to God—this is your true and proper worship."*

Let's consider the story of Daniel from the Bible. Daniel sets an excellent example for us when it comes to the health of our bodies. King Nebuchadnezzar requested to bring into his service some young men without any physical defect, handsome, showing an aptitude for every kind of learning, well informed, quick to understand, and qualified to serve in the king's palace. Essentially, studly dudes. Daniel was selected as one of the men who were to be trained to serve. Nebuchadnezzar assigned them a daily amount of food and wine from his table. Daniel asked for and was granted permission to have nothing but vegetables to eat and water to drink for ten days. At the end of this period, Daniel and the other men involved in this practice looked healthier and better nourished than the young men who ate the royal food. (Daniel 1:8-16)

Although God doesn't want us to become obsessive about our bodies, he does want us to be good stewards of our health. In *The Daniel Plan*, Rick Warren says that what you do with your body sets the tone for everything else. Physical health influences your mental health, spiritual health, emotional health, and relational health. If you are worth dying for, don't you think God wants you to take good care of yourself?

Below are some good practices for taking care of your "temple:"

Eat well

You've heard the phrase "you are what you eat." It's kind of true. Food is fuel, and we need it to function optimally. Eating well means feeding your body what it needs. You know what to do! Eat lots of fruits and vegetables. Watch your portion sizes. Limit processed foods and sugar.

Hydrate

Drink lots of water and stay hydrated! Most sources recommend sixty-four ounces of water a day. I can't quite get there with my old lady bladder, but I try!

Get sufficient sleep

A good night's sleep is essential. Sleep gives your body a chance to restore and regenerate. Seven to eight hours per day is recommended for most adults.

Get moving

Sedentary behavior has been linked to a wide range of medical problems and a shorter lifespan. Get up and move during the day. Exercise often, doing something you enjoy so you will stick with it.

Don't smoke or use tobacco products

If you want to live an enjoyable life, don't smoke or chew tobacco. The list of diseases and cancers attributed to tobacco use is extensive.

REFLECT

- Are you doing a good job taking care of your temple?
- What are you doing that's positive? What do you need to change to best honor your temple?

_____
_____
_____
_____
_____
_____
_____
_____
_____
_____
_____
_____
_____
_____
_____
_____
_____
_____
_____
_____
_____
_____
_____
_____
_____

Making Change Happen

With each new year, many of us set New Year's resolutions. We resolve to lose weight, exercise, manage our finances better, eat healthier, and read our Bible more, to name a few. Have you ever made New Year's resolutions that didn't stick? According to *U.S. News & World Report*, the failure rate for New Year's resolutions is about eighty percent, and most lose their resolve by mid-February. I know for sure that, many more times than not, my resolutions have failed.

So, why aren't we better at making and keeping our resolutions? Sources cite any number of issues to explain the massive rate of failure. Everything from lack of clarity to setting expectations too high. Another source I read said that the psychology behind the word "resolution" itself is a problem. Resolution is a strong, demanding word that indicates that there is no room for failure. However, we are human, and some amount of failure is inevitable.

The real problem is within our hearts and minds. We'd all like to be better people, but no matter how hard we try, we find ourselves tripped up by our moral failures and weaknesses. Even the Apostle Paul experienced this. He said, *"For I have the desire to do what is good, but I cannot carry it out"* (Romans 7:18).

We seem to think that the New Year is the only time we can set out to make changes. However, we can do it at any time! Below are some tips to make positive changes stick, any time of year.

Understand that you can't, but God can

We usually try to successfully make changes based on our own willpower. Seeking to make those changes in our power generally doesn't work and also dishonors God. The best strategy for keeping our resolutions rests in total dependence on Him.

Zechariah 4:6 says, *"...Not by might nor power, but by my Spirit..."*

Philippians 4:13 says, *"I can do all this through him who gives me strength."* *This means we must depend on His strength continuously to do all things, including changing our behaviors.*

Connect with God and others

It can be extremely helpful to include God and a few close friends in identifying changes you would like to make and in holding you accountable.

Start with small changes

In my opinion, the key to long-lasting success is to develop new positive habits that replace the behaviors we want to change. One reason why we often fail is that we try to take on a big change at one time (i.e., change our entire diet, run a marathon). But, at the same time, we tend to resist extreme change. If something changes too rapidly, it's threatening, and we go back to what is comfortable. If your goal is to eat better, rather than going full force into a diet plan, pick small things you can change that can build into the larger change over time. Use a SMART goal format to formulate your bigger goals as well as the smaller things you will work on towards that end. This means that your goals should be specific, measurable, achievable, relevant, and time-bound.

The Apostle Paul experienced more than his fair share of failure during his life. During one of his stints in prison, he wrote about his unwillingness to give up. *"Forgetting what is behind and straining toward what is ahead, I press on toward the goal to win the prize for which God has called me heavenward in Christ Jesus"* (Philippians 3:13b-14).

Paul stopped looking back and looked forward instead. He didn't let the fear of failure hold him back. We can reflect on this when we feel like giving up on the changes we seek to make.

REFLECT

- What are some behaviors that you would like to change over the coming weeks?
- What small changes can you make towards your bigger goals?

Confessions of a Hot Mess- from MESS to MESSage

Loving Yourself

Do you love yourself? Many people may hesitate to say "yes" because we often think self-love is prideful, arrogant, and even narcissistic. However, the Bible indicates that it is proper and necessary to love yourself to a reasonable degree, but not in those worldly ways. The type of love that God wants you to have for yourself is based upon humility and thankfulness. You should care for yourself, respect yourself, and appreciate the person that God has made in you.

I remember a period in my life where I was going to a counselor, and I told her that I had a persistent, underlying feeling that nothing I did was good enough. Not good, right? And I didn't even realize that I was feeling that way until our session. Luckily, she helped me to move past it, although admittedly, I still struggle. I'm sure that I'm not alone in struggling with loving—or even liking—myself at times.

Whom should we love first? Here's what the Bible tells us:

Jesus says the most important commandment is: *"Love the Lord your God with all your heart and with all your soul and with all your mind and with all your strength"* (Mark 12:30).

Further, he says the second is this: *"Love your neighbor as yourself"* (Mark 12:31).

Although the Bible doesn't tell us specifically to love ourselves, it is certainly implied here. Think about it; you can't give away something you don't have in yourself. How can you love others if you don't even love yourself?

Many of us are in bondage as it relates to how we feel about ourselves. Maybe you consider yourself ugly, dumb, clumsy, lazy, or all of the above. Maybe you are ashamed and haven't forgiven yourself for things you have done in the past. Maybe you have low self-esteem and see yourself as a failure or as less than others around you. Maybe you regularly beat up on yourself mentally or emotionally.

I remember my daughter asking me during her tween years, "Mom, why did God—and you and dad—make me ugly?" And then, she added that her friend said she looked like me and further reiterated that resembling me was not a good thing. So then, I wasn't loving myself too much. We may sometimes ask questions like this and wonder why we aren't different or what we may perceive as better. But who are we to question how we are made? Clearly, God has a reason and certainly knows what He is doing. The Bible says that *"even the hairs of your head are all numbered" (Matthew 10:30 ESV).*

Here are some things to think about as it relates to loving ourselves:
- We were made in His image.
  - *"So God created man in his own image, in the image of God he created him; male and female he created them" (Genesis 1:27 ESV).*

- He knows each of us by name.
  - *"He calls his own sheep by name and leads them out" (John 10:3 NLT).*

- Before we were born, He knew us and set us apart for a purpose.
  - *"Before I formed you in the womb I knew you, before you were born I set you apart; I appointed you as a prophet to the nations" (Jeremiah 1:5).*

- And He lives inside each of us.
  - *"The Spirit of God has made me; the breath of the Almighty gives me life" (Job 33:4).*

God is a part of us, and He made each of us individually as part of His beautiful creation. He created us on purpose for a particular purpose. Who are we to question his creation? One of the things that helps me when I'm feeling a little down on myself is reading the Serenity Prayer:

"God grant me the serenity to accept the things I cannot change, courage to change those I can, and wisdom to know the difference."

There may be some things that you don't like about yourself that you can change. If so, ask God for the strength and support to make those changes. There are also likely things you can't change about yourself. Ask God to help you accept those things.

REFLECT

- Do you feel like you love yourself–in the Christian kind of way?
- If not, what can you do to increase your feelings of love for yourself?

Be with Someone Good for Your Soul

I saw the following quote on social media: "Be with someone who will take care of you. Not materialistically but take care of your soul, your well-being, your heart and everything that's you."

I was lucky enough to find and marry that person the second go around. He is a Christian man—quiet, kind, gentle, patient, and humble. And he can deal with my crazy. We are polar opposites on every assessment we take, but our relationship seems to work somehow. There are undoubtedly times when he frustrates me, probably because we are so different—and vice versa, I'm sure! But I feel that I can just be me and that he will always accept and love me for who I am, unconditionally.

The first go around, I think I unconsciously selected someone that I couldn't please because I never felt that I pleased my father. I guess I thought that if I could please my husband, I would be worthy. Ladies, many of us have gone into relationships thinking that we will change the other person. For those of us that are more seasoned, we haven't often seen that work. Only God can change a person.

My first marriage was difficult. I could never seem to do anything right in his eyes and felt constantly put down and criticized. The things that I didn't do right included vacuuming, laundry, parenting, and just about everything else around the house. By the time my marriage ended, my feelings about myself were not good, and I had pretty much hit rock bottom. When you have someone criticize and tear you down, day after day, it is exhausting. I realize that I wasn't perfect and did many things wrong in the relationship as well, but I did try to hold it together as long as I could. My parents had divorced, and I never wanted that for my children. But by the end of the marriage, there clearly wasn't another choice, and I was at peace with the decision.

Soon before we split up, I remember being at the beach with our family on what had been a difficult trip for me. My ex-husband was in rare form, and I knew things were falling apart. I woke up early one morning and sat on the deck to watch the sunrise. At that moment, I truly found Jesus and felt his support and encouragement. Up to that point, I had been attending church but was unsure about my faith.

Romans 8:28 speaks to me: *"And we know that in all things God works for the good of those who love him, who have been called according to his purpose."* God takes things that, in and of themselves, are bad, and He puts them together to bring healing. After we separated, things just kind of came together, and I could feel God working in my life and carrying me through. Our house sold quickly, and I found a great townhouse for the girls and me to live in. The timing worked out perfectly. In addition, after I'd had several years to heal, I truly believe that He brought my current husband into my life.

So, what's the point that I am trying to make in this chapter? I guess it's essentially the quote that I started with. Be with someone who is good for your soul. Now, if you don't have that and you are married, does that mean that you should get a divorce? That's not what I mean at all. Pray about it and ask God to help you improve the situation. If the relationship hasn't resulted in marriage, think about and pray about whether it's a healthy situation for you. And for younger ladies, don't decide to get married because everyone else is or you think your significant other is nice-looking–like I did. Go much deeper and pray about the situation.

REFLECT

- If you are currently married or in a serious relationship, reflect on it. If it isn't good for your soul, pray about it and let God comfort you and lead you in the way you should go.

_____
_____
_____
_____
_____
_____
_____
_____
_____
_____
_____
_____
_____

Say No to Emotional Abuse

Emotional abuse is any nonphysical behavior or attitude that controls, intimidates, subjugates, demeans, punishes, or isolates another person by using degradation, humiliation, or fear. (Beverly Engel, *The Emotionally Abusive Relationship*)

Imagine hearing the following on a regular basis:
- You are stupid.
- You are crazy.
- You are an unfit parent.
- You can't do anything right.
- I don't want you talking on the phone with your mother anymore.
- I wouldn't drink if it wasn't for you.
- It's none of your business where I've been. I just needed to get away from you.
- You are lucky you have me. No one else would want you.

Physical abuse is terrible, but at least you know that it's happening. Emotional abuse slowly chips away at your self-worth and kills your spirit. I was involved in an emotionally abusive relationship in the past. When it started, I stood my ground and fought back, but I began to lose track of reality over time. When being emotionally abused, you begin to ask yourself questions like: Am I really crazy? Am I actually an idiot? Maybe if I did this or that, things would be better.

Living within an abusive relationship is a slippery slope. I didn't fully realize that my relationship was abusive until I met with a counselor. I was trying to do everything that I could to preserve the relationship. I told her that I had been keeping a list of all the things I needed to change to make the relationship work. She asked me what he was doing to make things better, and this began to open my eyes.

Nowhere in Scripture does God condone any kind of abuse. In 1 Corinthians 13:4-7, God tells us that love is not rude, self-seeking, or easily angered. Further, He says that it keeps no record of wrongs and always protects. Malachi 2:16 says, "'The man who hates and divorces his wife,' says the Lord, the God of Israel, 'does violence to the one he should protect,' says the Lord Almighty. So be on your guard and do not be unfaithful."

I sincerely hope that no one reading this is currently in an emotionally abusive relationship. But if you are, there are some things that you can do to help the situation.

Set and enforce boundaries

Clearly state what you are willing to accept and what you are not. Let the abuser know the consequences if they don't adhere to your boundaries. Enforce the consequences every time the abuse occurs with no exceptions. Note that, when facing consequences, abusers often beg for forgiveness and promise to change. They may even mean what they say at the moment, but their true goal is to stay in control and keep you from leaving. If they return to the abusive behavior (which will likely happen), stick to your boundaries.

Build a support system

Abusers often will try to isolate you from others, but you must have a support system including family, clergy, friends, and neighbors.

Seek counseling

You and your spouse/significant other will need help to work through the challenges—as a couple, individually, or both.

Pray and trust God!

Pray for the relationship, your spouse/significant other, and yourself! Ask God to guide you on the next steps and carry you through, whatever the outcome.

If you are/have been the victim of emotional abuse, please know you are not alone. And, even more importantly, know that God can and will bring you healing.

> *"And the God of all grace, who called you to his eternal glory in Christ, after you have suffered a little while, will himself restore you and make you strong, firm and steadfast" (1 Peter 5:10).*

REFLECT

- Are you—or have you ever been—in an emotionally abusive relationship? If so, how could you use the information shared to help in healing?

- Do you know anyone else that is in an emotionally abusive relationship? How could you support and care for her/him?

Breaking Through Our Busy

"Come to me, all you who are weary and burdened, and I will give you rest. Take my yoke upon you and learn from me, for I am gentle and humble in heart, and you will find rest for your souls. For my yoke is easy and my burden is light" (Matthew 11:28-30).

Have you noticed that being busy is seen as a badge of honor in our society? And we sometimes even see it as a sign of importance. The year 2020 was certainly a wake-up call for many of us. Maybe it was partially God's way of telling us to chill out!

My husband and I have four kids between us, and I worked full-time outside the home as they were growing up. Boy, do I know busy. The kids were all involved in activities, so it seemed that there was somewhere to go most evenings. Not to mention figuring out dinner, doing laundry, cleaning the house, and squeezing in time to exercise. There was always something that needed to be done. If I sat down for very long, I'd start feeling guilty that I wasn't being productive. I was so tired that I would fall into bed each night.

Let's consider the story of Mary and Martha in Luke 10:38-42:

> As Jesus and his disciples were on their way, he came to a village where a woman named Martha opened her home to him. She had a sister called Mary, who sat at the Lord's feet listening to what he said. But Martha was distracted by all the preparations that had to be made. She came to him and asked, "Lord, don't you care that my sister has left me to do the work by myself? Tell her to help me!" "Martha, Martha," the Lord answered, "you are worried and upset about many things, but few things are needed—or indeed only one. Mary has chosen what is better and it will not be taken away from her."

Are you a Mary or a Martha? If I polled ten women, I'll bet that there would be a lot more Martha's than Mary's. I know for sure that I'd be a Martha. First of all, I probably would have never invited Jesus and his followers into my home because I hate to entertain. I always feel like things have to be perfect and get stressed out. Secondly, imagine the pressure of having Jesus Christ, the Son of God, at your house! I'm sure I'd also be scurrying around and getting miffed at

Mary for not helping me.

I think that we, as women, are somewhat conditioned to serve others and often take things on ourselves that aren't always necessary. We value getting things done and keep ourselves constantly on the move doing things with and for family, children, work, school, community, and church. Plus, our minds are constantly spinning, trying to keep our schedule and commitments straight, while we have a constant influx of information from the media and the internet to process.

Although Martha was working diligently to serve others (which certainly isn't a bad thing), she wasn't focused on what was most important–Jesus and his presence. Other things have a way of working out and falling into place when our primary focus is on Him. In Matthew 6:33 (BSB), Jesus says, *"But seek first the kingdom of God and His righteousness, and all these things will be added unto you."*

Getting your other priorities clear is essential to helping you to lead a more balanced, less busy life. Ask yourself, "What are my main things?"

- If you could focus on one thing and one thing only, what would that be? - Hint, this one should be God.
- If you could add a second thing, what would that be?
- A third?
- A fourth?
- A fifth?

Now that you know your priorities, consider dropping any commitments and pursuits that aren't on your list. Here are some other strategies that you might consider to better balance your life.

Outsource

Hire or recruit others to take care of some of your tasks so that you can focus on what's most meaningful.

Bundle

Kill two birds with one stone (i.e., volunteer for a community service activity where you will also get some exercise).

Learn to say no

Consider saying no to things that don't fit in with your priorities.

Delegate tasks

Delegate tasks at work and home when possible. Make the kids and spouse help out! Regrettably, I didn't do very well with this.

Manage your time

Some suggestions include:
- Organizing household tasks efficiently
- Running errands in batches where possible
- Relaxing your cleaning standards
- Keeping a weekly calendar of important dates and daily to-dos

Get enough sleep

A good night's sleep is a gift from God (Psalm 127:2). And Jesus himself was not opposed to getting some shuteye, even when a severe storm threatened him and his disciples.

REFLECT

- Determine your top five priorities and think about commitments that you might adjust or drop.
- Which of the strategies listed could you use to obtain a better balance?

_____
_____
_____
_____
_____
_____
_____
_____
_____
_____
_____
_____
_____
_____
_____

10

Self-Care is Not Selfish

When we think of self-care, we often visualize images of massages, facials, spas, and luxurious bath products. We tend to view self-care as an indulgence. But it's not; it's essential to our well-being. So, what exactly is self-care? It involves being mindful of our limits and needs to ensure our physical, emotional, and mental well-being.

I'm pretty good at self-care in my current season of life, but that wasn't always the case. I, like many women, tried to take care of everyone else and often neglected myself as it was hard to fit anything else into my overflowing schedule. You have probably heard that we can't give what we don't have, which is true when it comes to caring for others. If we don't take time to care for ourselves, our well will run dry, and our ability to care for and help others will be diminished.

At its core, self-care is all about being good stewards of our bodies and souls so that we can be our best selves. We are God's handiwork (fearfully and wonderfully made), and He wants us to flourish and thrive, not be depleted and exhausted. Jesus prioritized self-care in his life as indicated below:

Many times in the Bible, Jesus retreated from everyone else to rest alone or pray. (Mark 1:9-13, Mark 1:35, Mark 6:30-32, Mark 6:45-46)

Jesus took time to sleep, even in the midst of chaos. (Matthew 8:23-27)

Jesus encouraged Martha not to be anxious about doing housework but to come and relax with him as Mary had done. (Luke 10:38-42)

Jesus surrounded himself with close friends who would fellowship with him and encourage Him.

When I speak about self-care, I don't mean binging on Netflix while eating a chocolate bar and drinking wine, although I do enjoy these things. Self-care emphasizes developing personal habits and practices to manage your health and reduce stress and anxiety. Some of these practices are listed below. We have already talked about many of these, but the fact that they keep coming up emphasizes the importance of these habits.

Eat healthy and exercise

> "Do you not know that your bodies are temples of the Holy Spirit, who is in you, whom you have received from God? You are not your own; you were bought at a price. Therefore honor God with your bodies" (1 Corinthians 6:19-20).

Give yourself space to connect with God and prioritize time with Him

> "But Jesus often withdrew to lonely places and prayed" (Luke 5:16).

Do things you enjoy and have fun

> "That each of them may eat and drink, and find satisfaction in all their toil--this is the gift of God" (Ecclesiastes 3:13).

Rest regularly

> "By the seventh day God had finished the work he had been doing; so on the seventh day he rested from all his work. Then God blessed the seventh day and made it holy, because on it he rested from all the work of creating that he had done" (Genesis 2:2-3).

Spend time in nature

> "The heavens declare the glory of God; the skies proclaim the work of his hands" (Psalm 19:1b).

Engage in preventive care activities

Just the other day, I went to the dentist, got a mammogram, and went to the "mole patrol" (dermatologist). Many self-care habits are not fun, but they are critical to your health and well-being.

So next time you think you don't have time for self-care, realize that you don't have time NOT to practice self-care. Not sure if that made sense, but you know what I mean. Let's end with this Scripture which always brings me comfort.

Jesus said, "Are you tired? Worn out? Burned out on religion? Come to me. Get away with me and you'll recover your life. I'll show you how to take a real rest. Walk with me and work with me—watch how I do it. Learn the unforced rhythms of grace. I won't lay anything heavy or ill-fitting on you. Keep company with me and you'll learn to live freely and lightly" (Matthew 11:28-30 MSG).

REFLECT

- How would you rate your self-care on a scale of 1 to 10?
- What do you need to do to ensure that you are caring for yourself adequately?

_____
_____
_____
_____
_____
_____
_____
_____
_____
_____
_____
_____
_____
_____
_____
_____
_____
_____
_____
_____
_____
_____
_____
_____
_____
_____

Leslie Speas

Section 2:

Loving and Caring for Others

LESLIE SPEAS

Love Your Neighbor as Yourself

"For the entire law is fulfilled in keeping this one command: 'Love your neighbor as yourself'" (Galatians 5:14).

I have most often thought of love as being a romantic or emotional feeling towards someone. The Christian love of the Bible, *agape* love, means affection, high esteem, or concern for the welfare of another person. It is a deliberate, purposeful love. "Love your neighbor as yourself" is probably one of the more well-known verses in the Bible. In fact, it is mentioned eight times!

I think that I am typically a caring and compassionate person but do I always "love my neighbors" even when I don't like them? I wish I could say yes, but that's not always the case. It's hard to imagine how we can be expected to love someone who is hateful or disrespectful to us. How can we learn to love the grumpy neighbor that yells at us to keep our dog off his lawn when we don't even like him? Or the coworker that throws us under the bus or stabs us in the back?

"Love your neighbor" is not as hard as it sounds on the surface. It simply means respecting others and regarding their needs and desires as highly as we regard our own. The secret is to think of the other person as someone as worthy of God's love as we are. We are all part of God's creation, and He sees us all as His children.

Who is our neighbor? Is it the guy or girl next door? Could it be someone in our community or someone we work with? Jesus says that it is all of these. It could even be someone that we don't know that we come across when running errands.

The parable of the Good Samaritan (Luke 10) shows us what it means to love your neighbor. In this parable, a man is beaten and left half-dead on the side of the road. While he lies there helpless, a priest and later a Levite see him and deliberately walk on. Finally, a Samaritan sees the victim and responds by helping him.

Jesus gives us this instruction:

"Which of these three do you think was a neighbor to the man who fell into the hands of robbers?" The expert in the law replied, "The one who had mercy on him." Jesus told him, "Go and do likewise" (Luke 10:36-37).

Here is some information that may be helpful in the quest to love your neighbors.

<u>Always show respect to others</u>

We should respect others because God said to. For example, we read in the Bible that husbands and wives are to respect one another: *"However, each of you must also love his wife as he loves himself, and the wife must respect her husband" (Ephesians 5:33).*

The same principle applies to other relationships. Even if someone has disrespected you, he or she is a child of God and, as such, deserving of respect.

<u>Show compassion</u>

In Proverbs 31:8-9, the Bible defines compassion as follows: *"Speak up for those who cannot speak for themselves, for the rights of all who are destitute. Speak up and judge fairly; defend the rights of the poor and needy."* The Samaritan could have kept walking after seeing the man's need, but he felt compassion for the man and acted on it. We all get busy, and it's easy to overlook the needs of others. We sometimes just keep on walking even after we feel compassion. If you feel it, act on it! Think about who God is placing on your heart and show compassion to him or her.

<u>Try to know and understand others better</u>

Make every effort to know and understand others better--their hopes, fears, concerns, and aspirations. We don't know what the others are going through. Maybe they are depressed or lonely. Maybe they have recently lost a loved one or a job. Maybe the love you show them will make a difference in their lives and make things a little bit better for them or give them some hope! I like to think that there is some good in all of us—and, as mentioned before, we are all children of God who He loves.

<u>Understand that love is sacrificial and often inconvenient</u>

In the parable of the Good Samaritan, the Samaritan gave two denarii to the innkeeper to help the man, and no payback was expected in return. In addition to giving our material resources, loving others takes our time, which is a precious commodity. However, God has instructed us to love our neighbor, even when it's costly, inconvenient, or messy.

Confessions of a Hot Mess- from MESS to MESSage

I love me some C.S. Lewis. He said, "Do not waste time wondering whether you "love" your neighbor, act as if you did. As soon as we do this, we find one of the greatest secrets. When you are behaving as if you love someone, you will presently come to love him."

REFLECT

- Take some time to think about how you can love your neighbors. Be on the lookout for opportunities to help and "love" others. When God places someone on your heart, listen and do it!

12

Love Your Enemies - Wait, What?

"But I tell you, love your enemies and pray for those who persecute you" (Matthew 5:44).

We've talked about loving our neighbor. We are further instructed to love our enemies. Wait, what? I'm still trying to work on forgiving my enemies—loving them is a definite stretch. As was mentioned previously, the word love has many different meanings. I came across a definition that I liked in this context: I affirm and respect you, and I wish you well. We don't have to add our enemies to our Christmas list, but we can try to love them in this way and forgive them, knowing that this is what we need to do for God and ourselves.

And we are asked to pray for our persecutors? I don't think this includes the prayer, "Please give that person what's coming to them." I have said that one a time or two. We are asked to sincerely pray for them and their well-being.

I read that it's important to understand that our offenders are victims in their own way, and the hurt they spew is probably more of a reflection of their insecurities than a reflection on us. Our real enemy is Satan, who keeps tempting all of us to do wrong.

To love our enemies, we first have to forgive them. Matthew 6:14-15 (NLT) says, *"If you forgive those who sin against you, your heavenly Father will forgive you. But if you refuse to forgive others, your Father will not forgive your sins."*

If God can forgive us for our sins, we should be able to forgive others! But what about mean girls? I can tell you that there are still a few from back in the day that I harbor some bad feelings toward and wouldn't look forward to seeing at a reunion. What about bullies and backstabbers? Most of us have encountered them at some point, when we were young and as adults in the workplace, and maybe even in church. It's especially hard for me to imagine forgiving someone who wronged or harmed me or a loved one in an extreme way, such as through sexual abuse or even death.

I (as I'm sure is the case for many of us) have struggled with forgiveness at times during my life. We have all been hurt by others, and it can be challenging to get past the hurt, forgive, and move on. My mother held on to bitterness and resentment towards my dad for his actions, resulting in their divorce, for many years. I'm pretty sure she still did even forty years later as she commented that he was "dead to her." My mother was a little dark. She ended up remarrying someone with whom she was much happier, but her life was always tainted by bitterness.

Forgiveness is defined as a conscious, deliberate decision to release feelings of resentment or vengeance toward a person or group who has harmed you, regardless of whether they deserve your forgiveness. Forgiveness benefits us and is critical to our happiness and growth. When we hold onto hurt, pain, resentment, and anger, it harms us much more than it does the other person. Some of the last words that Jesus uttered were, *"Father, forgive them, for they know not what they do"* (Luke 23:34 ESV).

Consider this story from Matthew 18:21-22 (BSB):

> *Then Peter came to Jesus and asked, "Lord, how many times shall I forgive my brother who sins against me? Up to seven times?" Jesus answered, "I tell you, not just seven times, but seventy-seven times!"*

That's a lot of times. I think it means as many as it takes. Often, we may not feel like forgiving someone. It's important to understand that forgiveness doesn't necessarily excuse wrongdoings. It's not a pardon or condoning what the other person has done. Forgive and forget is not a biblical quote. Forgiving doesn't negate the pain or reverse things that have happened; it just frees you from the burden of hatred and bitterness. Choosing not to forgive gets us stuck in our past, preventing us from moving forward.

As we have seen, the Bible takes it beyond forgiveness and tells us to "love our enemies." Luke 6:27-29 says,

> *But I tell you who hear me: Love your enemies, do good to those who hate you, bless those who curse you, pray for those who mistreat you. If someone strikes you on one cheek, turn to him the other also. If someone takes your cloak, do not stop him from taking your tunic.*

In summary, here are some key points that may help us to forgive and love our enemies:

- Understand that to forgive doesn't mean we have to forget. We are simply letting go of the past and moving forward. As long as we have unforgiveness in our hearts, we will be separated from God.

- Remember that if God can forgive us for the bad stuff we've done, we should forgive others. Romans 3:23 (ASV) says, "for all have sinned and fall short of the glory of God..."

- Consider that our "enemies" are fellow human beings and children of God who he loves. We should do our best to show them respect and compassion.

* Write a letter of forgiveness to the person (not necessarily to give or mail to them, though you could), letting them know that you forgive them. Sometimes just writing out the message is therapeutic in its own right.

If you are having trouble forgiving someone, pray about it and ask God for His help. You may also want to talk to a friend or spiritual counselor who may be able to help you move forward.

Let's end with this quote from Nelson Mandela: "As I walked out the door toward the gate that would lead to my freedom, I knew if I didn't leave my bitterness and hatred behind, I'd still be in prison."

REFLECT

* Is there someone in your life that you haven't forgiven?
* What steps could you take towards forgiveness?
* How do you feel about being instructed to "love your enemies"? What does that mean to you?

_____
_____
_____
_____
_____
_____
_____
_____
_____
_____
_____
_____
_____
_____
_____
_____

13
Be Quick to Listen and Slow to Speak

"My dear brothers and sisters, take note of this: Everyone should be quick to listen, slow to speak and slow to become angry, because human anger does not produce the righteousness that God desires" (James 1:19-20).

We could all probably benefit from being better listeners. I know that I am often guilty of listening to respond rather than actually listening to hear and attend to the other person's heart. And I sometimes just straight up don't listen. My hubby works in Information Technology and often likes to tell me about his day when he gets home from work in the evening. He talks to me about things like firewalls and motherboards, which aren't even in my vocabulary. I often tune him out, and he has noticed. We joke that what I hear is kind of like the teacher in Charlie Brown, which sounds like "whomp whomp whomp."

To listen attentively, we have to minimize distractions, turn off the voice in our minds, and truly focus on hearing the other person. When we do these things, we are better equipped to be compassionate and understanding and make the other person feel valued.

In addition to listening, we are instructed to be slow to speak. I don't know about you, but there have been many times when I should have practiced the pause before I said something. Proverbs is full of advice for us on this topic:

- *"When words are many, sin is not absent, but he who holds his tongue is wise"* (10:19).

- *"He who answers a matter before he hears it—this is folly and disgrace to him"* (18:13 BSB).

- *"She speaks with wisdom, and faithful instruction is on her tongue"* (31:26).

I'm quite far from being like the Proverbs 31 woman in the verse above, but I will try to continue to focus on being slower and more thoughtful before I speak. I do fairly well in interacting with others outside of my family but not so much with my family members. Just the other day, I contemplated having a conversation with my daughter about an issue that I felt the need to advise her on. I had three reminders (devotions, podcasts, Facebook posts) about being "slow to speak" and "holding my tongue." I think this was likely guidance not to say anything, but I had to go and do it anyway! And, shocker, it didn't go well. Shouldn't we treat our family members with as much respect, kindness, and love (if not more) than others? Another thing I'm working on.

The THINK acronym provides a great guideline to influence our speech. It helps us to parse out words that may be angry, hurtful, or negative:

> **T** is it true?
>
> **H** is it helpful?
>
> **I** is it inspiring?
>
> **N** is it necessary?
>
> **K** is it kind?

Here are a few reminders from the Bible to reflect on as we conclude this chapter:

"Do not let any unwholesome talk come out of your mouths, but only what is helpful for building others up according to their needs, that it may benefit those who listen" (Ephesians 4:29).

Okay, this one bothers me: *"A quarrelsome wife is as annoying as constant dripping on a rainy day"* (Proverbs 19:13 NLT). I may be guilty of nagging once in a while. Next time you are tempted to nag or say something unkind, replace it with the prayer, "Bless him/her, change me."

REFLECT

- We could all benefit from becoming better listeners. What will you do to improve your ability to really listen and attend to the other person's heart?
- Do you need to be "slower to speak" at times? What could you do to help yourself practice the pause?

CONFESSIONS OF A HOT MESS- FROM MESS TO MESSAGE

14

More on Listening

I think listening is one of the most important skills we can have, so I wanted to spend a little more time on the topic. As I said, I have my challenges with listening, particularly if it's a topic I don't care very much about (like computers or most sports), or the other person goes on too long. We all have that person in our life!

I was having dinner the other night with some friends. According to the wives, two of the husbands have recently contracted a hearing disorder that sounded like "selective listening" to me. My husband has that too, sometimes. And, if I'm honest, I do too. Most of us have had training at one time or another on active listening, but we don't tend to do it very well.

Below are some steps that you can take to be a better listener based on the acronym LISTEN. Clever, right? I must admit I didn't come up with this on my own. I borrowed and adapted it from Pastor Rick's Daily Hope podcast featuring Rick Warren:

L ook and listen with your body language
- Use your eye contact, body language, and gestures to convey your attention.

I nvest in the interaction
- Give the speaker your undivided attention and focus on receiving the intended message.
- Avoid distractions and multi-tasking, and don't mentally prepare your rebuttal.

S hare their feelings, not your solution
- As a listener, your role is to understand what is being said, not to impose your solution.
- Summarize the other person's comments and feelings as you understand them.

T une into any underlying feelings or issues

- Tune into their body language and try to identify any underlying issues that aren't apparent through what they are saying verbally.

E ngage the speaker with open-ended questions
- Ask open-ended follow-up questions to clarify, show interest, and increase your understanding.

N ever judge until you have all the information
- Don't jump to conclusions or make judgments until you have listened to the entire message.

Of course, Proverbs shares some additional wisdom on listening.

"The way of fools seems right to them, but the wise listen to advice" (Proverbs 12:15).

"...turning your ear to wisdom and applying your heart to understanding..." (Proverbs 2:2).

REFLECT

- On a scale of 1 to 10, how would you rate yourself on being a good listener?
- What will you do to improve your ability to listen well?

_____
_____
_____
_____
_____
_____
_____
_____
_____
_____
_____
_____
_____
_____

15

Find Yourself by Serving Others

"Each one should use whatever gift he has received to serve others, as faithful stewards of God's grace in its various forms" (1 Peter 4:10).

I truly believe that joy in life is found when we stop making life about ourselves and start making it about other people. Life is so much better when we are loving and serving others!

I have been blessed to have the opportunity to mentor a young woman, Ashley, from a local non-profit high school that focuses on giving high-risk youth a second chance. I visited the school as a potential recruiting source for my employer at the time and fell in love with their Christian-based approach to helping youth. From there, I joined their board and got connected with mentoring a student.

Ashley is an amazing young woman who hasn't had the advantages in life that many of us have had. She has a young son and recently married her son's dad. I was very involved in planning her wedding, which is a little scary because those who know me are aware that this type of thing is not in my wheelhouse. Something I read said that the Lord doesn't call the equipped; he equips the called. That is definitely the case here!

The wedding was held at my church. The event was small and had no budget. However, I think it turned out very nice. Some of my friends and neighbors pitched in to provide food, flowers, and decorations. I was amazed by the people that were willing to donate their time, talents, and resources. I am blessed with such kind and caring people in my life who would reach out to help someone that they don't know.

Mentoring and helping this young woman has truly been one of the most meaningful things I have done in a long time. This experience has helped me to see that "the best way to find yourself is to lose yourself in the service to others" (Mahatma Gandhi).

In 1 Peter 5:5 (GNT), we are instructed to *"put on the apron of humility"* to serve one another. Jesus measured greatness in terms of service, not by the world's standards of wealth, power, and position. He shaped us for service, not self-centeredness. I know that I've been guilty in the past of having excuses for not helping others like: I don't have time; I don't know what to do; I don't have any special skills to contribute.

There have also been times when I have wanted to help others and be more involved in the community but wasn't sure what to do or what organizations would fit me. I prayed about it, and I truly believe that God brought me to the school and Ashley.

I feel that I have found my calling to serve where I can use my strengths and maybe leverage other's strengths as I did with Ashley's wedding. I hope to continue to keep my eyes off myself and focus on loving and helping others.

> *"Let each of you look not only to your own interests, but also to the interests of others" (Philippians 2:4 MEV).*

REFLECT

* What are you doing to serve others?
* If you are looking for additional opportunities to serve, look around you at your workplace/community/church. Pray about it, and let God lead you to opportunities to serve.

_____
_____
_____
_____
_____
_____
_____
_____
_____
_____
_____
_____
_____
_____
_____
_____
_____

16

Who Are We to Judge?

Do not judge, or you too will be judged. For in the same way you judge others, you will be judged, and with the measure you use, it will be measured to you. Why do you look at the speck of sawdust in your brother's eye and pay no attention to the plank in your own eye? How can you say to your brother, 'Let me take the speck out of your eye,' when all the time there is a plank in your own eye? You hypocrite, first take the plank out of your own eye, and then you will see clearly to remove the speck from your brother's eye (Matthew 7:1-5).

Some of us are experts at seeing what is wrong with others. We judge others for their shortcomings or the way they dress and talk. We even judge others for things that we ourselves are guilty of. Shocking, I know—but you know we all do it! We tend to think that our thoughts are right and anything that goes against them is wrong.

The passage above from Matthew is saying that we are incapable of seeing a person's heart or knowing his or her relationship with God, so we are not to take the place of God in making judgments about someone else. We should be humble, knowing that we too, have weaknesses and are guilty of sin.

Why do we judge? We may judge others because we aren't secure in ourselves, and it makes us feel a little better to tear others down. Or we may judge others because we think we know better, or maybe it's our pride or a lack of wisdom. I have seen judgment occur frequently—and have been guilty of it too—many times in my life. When I see people standing on the corner with a sign saying, "will work for food," I tend to make the judgment that they don't want to work and will spend any money they get on alcohol or drugs. This may be true in some instances, but I don't know that this is the case.

Recently, I saw judgment in action when I was out with my daughter and her boyfriend. My daughter has a very edgy look and most recently dyed her hair rainbow (which mom isn't too happy about). Her boyfriend has many tattoos, which isn't uncommon for their generation, but some of us older folks are still adapting. I seriously think tattoo removal will be big business at some point. I know that what I would have gotten tattooed on my body in my early 20s is probably not something I would want now. But I digress... I have noticed people looking at us and am pretty sure that they are making judgments about them. The truth is that my daughter is in Divinity School and plans to be a Youth Pastor, but most people would probably never think that based on her appearance.

There may be times in life when we are called to judge, like being on a jury or working in an area of the law. There are also times God calls on us to discern others' actions because of their potential impact on us. We may sometimes need to make judgments so we don't follow the wrong people. Matthew 24:24 (ESV) says, *"For false christs and false prophets will arise and perform great signs and wonders, so as to lead astray, if possible, even the elect."* The kind of judgment that is most damaging is self-righteous judging. This type of judging causes us to wrongly interpret what's going on with someone. We may think that another woman is stuck up or conceited because she is quiet and withdrawn. This woman could have a whole myriad of things going on that cause her to appear or come across a certain way. The reality is that we all have something difficult going on in our lives and we all are broken. Self-righteous judgment can also cause us to wrongly estimate ourselves and others based on blind spots or self-deception. John 7:24 says, *"Stop judging by mere appearances, and make a right judgment."*

Gossip is also a form of judgment that probably most of us have engaged in at one time or another. Who doesn't enjoy a little gossip once in a while? It can be interesting to share or hear a little dirt about someone, and it makes us feel just a little bit better about ourselves, right? The reality is that, by judging others in a hypocritical way, we damage our own lives by stealing our joy and peace as we know it's not the right thing to do. *"Do not judge, and you will not be judged. Do not condemn, and you will not be condemned. Forgive, and you will be forgiven"* (Luke 6:37).

Here are a few things you can do when you find yourself judging:

<u>Stop yourself</u>

Notice your thoughts and stop yourself when you find yourself being judgmental.

<u>Seek to understand the person</u>

Put yourself in the "judgee's" shoes, find out their story if you can, or imagine the circumstances that may have led them to act or look as they do.

<u>Accept the person</u>

Accept the person for who he/she is without trying to change him/her.

Love him or her

Love the other person as a brother or sister, a fellow child of God, regardless of their age, the color of their skin, their sex, or social status.

I've started using these tips when I find myself judging—and yes, I am still a work in progress!

REFLECT

- Are you sometimes guilty of judging? Be honest!
- What is a recent example of a time you judged someone else?
- What can you do to work towards overcoming this tendency to judge others?

_____
_____
_____
_____
_____
_____
_____
_____
_____
_____
_____
_____
_____
_____
_____
_____
_____
_____
_____
_____

Build 'Em Up

"Anxiety weighs down the heart, but a kind word cheers it up" (Proverbs 12:25).

We are around people every day—at work, at home, at school, at church, and when we are out and about. Many of these people are struggling due to the words and actions of others, even going back to when they were children. It is important for us, as Christians, to work to build others up instead of tearing them down.

At work, I advise leaders regularly to recognize employees and ensure they feel valued. Numerous studies and pure common sense indicate that this is extremely important to employee motivation and engagement. I have found that this is generally an opportunity for improvement across various workplaces that I have been involved with. People often don't take the time to build others up. If they did, it would pay great dividends in terms of work performance and teamwork. I know people that have kept thank you notes that they have received from someone at work for years, and many even have them posted in their workspace. In fact, I found a few notes in my "workbox" that I have taken from job to job and that I haven't had the heart to get rid of. I may be a bit of a job hopper.

We often celebrate and say nice things about people as they leave a job, retire, or relocate. Why not say and do things to recognize and encourage them while they are still around? The same could be said when people die. Why do we wait until they are gone to say good things about them?

It is necessary and helpful at times to give others feedback on how they can improve. I have heard different statistics on how much positive feedback is needed to counteract corrective feedback. Sources say anywhere from three to six. It's kind of like a bank account. You make a deposit with each positive interaction and make a much greater withdrawal with each negative interaction. That means if we ever give correction or feedback for improvement, we need to be at least three to six times as good at encouraging and speaking positively. Yet another reason why it's important to build others up!

I have always done pretty well with building others up at work, but not as much in my personal relationships. There have been times when I have found myself being critical of friends or family members because they didn't act or do things like I thought they should. Sometimes, I'm not even conscious that I'm doing this until after the fact. And sometimes I make critical comments that add absolutely no value—but I go ahead and do it anyway.

Let's look at some words that can tear others down.
- Gossip – We talked about gossip already. It involves sharing negative information about others to tear down their reputation.
- Destructive criticism – Criticism or feedback that is just mean and is meant to diminish or discredit another.
- Slanderous words - Lies or half-truths directed at destroying someone's reputation and damaging their relationships with others.
- Angry words – Words and name-calling that hurt others.

"Do not let any unwholesome talk come out of your mouths, but only what is helpful for building others up according to their needs, that it may benefit those who listen" (Ephesians 4:29).

We are like a house that can be torn down or built up. It is so easy for us to speak words that hurt, criticize, or tear each other down. Instead, we should build each other up by using words of grace. Speaking words of grace involves encouragement, expressions of concern, and words of blessing and praise. We all like to hear things like:
- "I appreciate you."
- "I love you."
- "Thank you for what you did to help me."
- "You did a great job."
- "How can I help you?"
- "I am praying for you."
- "You have inspired me."

When we share words of grace, it also makes us feel good because we have encouraged someone or made them feel better. Proverbs 11:25 (NLT) says, *"…those who refresh others will themselves be refreshed."*

We should follow the example of Barnabas, who excelled in encouraging others and was even nicknamed *"son of encouragement" (Acts 4:36)*. He was a good man in the early church who showed kindness, generosity, and a forgiving nature to others and helped to encourage many. He wanted to see the church grow and flourish and did all he could to make this happen.

We should try to make encouraging others a daily practice. For some of us it comes naturally, but not as much for others. If it doesn't come naturally for you, schedule time for "building others up" on your calendar or send yourself other reminders. Send a text, give them a call, write a handwritten note, share kind words, whatever works for you. Be a light in a too often dim world!

"Therefore encourage one another and build each other up, just as in fact you are doing" (1 Thessalonians 5:11).

REFLECT

- How can you make building up others a daily part of your routine?
- What obstacles are keeping you from doing this, and how can you get around them?

18
Constructive Criticism

"Listen to my instruction and be wise. Don't ignore it" (Proverbs 8:33 NLT).

Most of us don't enjoy correction as it makes us feel like we have done something wrong. It can be difficult to receive graciously because it may hurt our feelings or our pride. However, correction is necessary for us to learn and grow. At work, I teach that constructive feedback is a gift. And it is because it helps us get better.

I have struggled with handling corrective feedback for most of my life. I am receptive to it, but then I beat myself up. I have gotten better at it as I have gotten older and wiser (ha! not sure about that second part)–but admittedly, I still struggle.

I have also observed that many people also hesitate to give corrective feedback. Some of the reasons are as follows:

- They want to be nice.
- They don't want to hurt anyone's feelings.
- They aren't sure how it will be received and want to avoid conflict.

It's important to give correction when appropriate to help others. However, it must come from a place of caring and concern. When it doesn't, it's generally hurtful and not well received. First Corinthians 4:14 supports this idea: *"I am writing this not to shame you but to warn you as my dear children."*

Below are some tips for giving and receiving correction:

<u>*When giving correction:*</u>

- Ask clarifying questions to gain a more accurate understanding. Don't assume you know everything.
- Be graciously frank. Don't hint, beat around the bush, or over-qualify. Say what you see with the humility that you might not be seeing things perfectly.

- Help to seek a solution that is good for everyone involved.
- Prepare what you are going to say and practice a little before giving corrective feedback.

When receiving correction:

- Don't deflect. Be open and humbly receive it.
- Listen to God's direction. God helps to cultivate our humility and will direct us in the way we should go.
- Try to see corrective feedback as a gift that will help you to learn and improve.

Scripture is the best source of instruction and correction in our lives. I know that it certainly has guided and corrected me a lot. Proverbs, in particular, sets me straight every time I read it. Here is an example: *"Whoever loves discipline loves knowledge, but he who hates correction is stupid"* (Proverbs 12:1 BSB).

"All Scripture is God-breathed and is useful for teaching, rebuking, correcting and training in righteousness, so that the servant of God may be thoroughly equipped for every good work" (2 Timothy 3:16-17).

REFLECT

- How are you at receiving correction?
- What about giving correction? What holds you back from giving it when appropriate?
- What things could you put into place to help you if you struggle with giving or receiving correction?

_____
_____
_____
_____
_____
_____
_____
_____
_____

Compassionate Conflict

Many people think conflict is bad. That isn't always the case. Conflict can be a productive and necessary part of any relationship. When managed biblically and compassionately, conflict can serve as a catalyst for change and an opportunity to grow a relationship.

I'm not particularly a lover of conflict. As I have gotten older, I have certainly become more mature in my approach to handling it. When I was younger, I would sometimes respond in anger in my personal relationships, often resulting in regret later. I was usually able to keep it together in my professional relationships but often just "stuffed" situations and didn't address them with the other person. This wasn't very productive and resulted in ongoing negative feelings towards the other party involved.

Here are some guidelines for compassionate conflict management:

<u>Before you respond to the situation:</u>

Take a break, think it through, and pray about your response. Doing this may prevent crucial mistakes in the relationship. Proverbs has some good advice that encourages us to take a pause. Consider these Scriptures:

- "A man's wisdom gives him patience; it is his glory to overlook an offense" (Proverbs 19:11).

- "Fools vent their anger, but the wise quietly hold it back" (Proverbs 29:11 NLT).

Think about whether it is worth your time and effort to address the situation. If they say something about "your mama," you know you have to address it... However, if it's something less controversial, it may behoove you to consider letting it go.

You should also reflect on your attitudes, strengths, and weaknesses and whether you have contributed to the situation. I know it's hard to believe, but sometimes the problem may be more about you than the other person.

If you are moving forward with addressing the conflict situation:

Press forward slowly, with forethought and self-control. Jesus provides us with direction for approaching someone in a conflict situation. In Matthew 18:15, Jesus said, *"If your brother or sister sins against you, go and point out their fault, just between the two of you. If they listen to you, you have won them over."* I believe this is an encouragement to go to the other person and speak with them alone—without sharing with others, without gossiping about it, and without trying to recruit others to your camp. This will provide a much better chance of restoring the relationship.

Below are some additional guidelines to use:

- **Plan a time** to discuss when you are both well-rested and in a good state of mind to be objective and show compassion to the other party.

- **Affirm the relationship** before clearly defining the problem. For example, "Our relationship is important to me, so I wanted to discuss something that has been on my mind with you. I feel hurt when you cancel the plans we have made at the last minute."

- **Clearly define the issue** and keep the discussion focused on it. I used to be especially good at dredging up all kinds of things from the past (and may still do this on occasion). It's best to stay focused and not rehash past issues or hurts.

- **Show compassion and kindness through your actions.** Once you share your feelings, lean in, and listen actively to the other person's perspective. Make sure that your body language, tone of voice, and other actions convey that you are open to their viewpoint. No eye-rolling, shrugging, or sighing allowed—even if you really want to! Summarize and reflect back to the individual what you believe you have heard.

- **Propose a solution.** When working toward a solution, consider Philippians 2:4-5 (BSB): *"Each of you should look not to your own interests, but also to the interests of others. Let this mind be in you which was also in Christ Jesus."* Strive for solutions that keep everyone's best interests in mind.

What if the other person isn't receptive to your efforts and/or willing to resolve the conflict? Then, as hard as it may be, forgive just as God in Christ has forgiven you. "Blessed are the peacemakers, for they will be called sons of God" (Matthew 5:9 BSB).

REFLECT

- Are you dealing with a current conflict that you need to resolve? If so, what steps will you take to move towards a resolution?

20

We All Bleed the Same

The song "Bleed the Same" by Mandisa speaks to me. Here are a few of the lyrics:

> *We all bleed the same*
> *We're more beautiful when we come together*
> *We all bleed the same*
> *So tell me why, tell me why we're divided*

Diversity includes all of the ways that we, as humans, are the same and different. People seem to notice and respond most quickly to race, gender, and age. These are obvious because they are visible, but there are many other dimensions of diversity, including religion, education, marital status, geographic location, and sexual orientation. Often, these differences create a divide between us. I have never understood why we can't appreciate our differences and get along. As humans, we have more commonalities than differences. As it says in the song, "we all bleed the same."

We should strive to create inclusive environments in our workplace, families, and communities where everyone respects one another regardless of differences, viewing differences as a good thing. I know the world would be a boring place if it was filled with a bunch of Leslies!

I'd like to think of the church as the most inclusive environment, but this isn't the case in many situations. In some church environments, people are rejected for various reasons, including the diverse differences listed above. Most recently, sexual orientation has been a big topic of discussion in the church. I have also always found it interesting that churches still seem to lack much racial/ethnic diversity. It seems that people often seem to choose to go to a church with people that look like them.

Biases and stereotypes impact our ability to leverage diversity and be inclusive. We don't like to think so, but we all have biases that have developed from sources such as the media, our education, our upbringing, our family, and our friends. We must be aware of potential biases that we may have internalized so we can mitigate any negative impact on our ability to be accepting and inclusive. We will explore biases in more detail in the next chapter.

Psalm 96:3-4 (ESV) says, *"Declare his glory among the nations, his marvelous works among all the peoples! For great is the Lord, and greatly to be praised; he is to be feared above all gods."* Notice this says, "all the peoples." In John 3:16, Jesus said, *"For God so loved the world that he gave his one and only Son, that whoever believes in him shall not perish but have eternal life."* "Whoever" means anyone who wants in!

Nothing in the New Testament that I have seen leads me to believe that there are any people who aren't worthy of God's love and don't deserve the human equality and inclusion that comes with that. As a matter of fact, Jesus tells his disciples in John 13:34, *"...Love one another. As I have loved you, so you must love one another."* Below are some additional Scriptures that show Jesus' views of inclusion.

> *"There is neither Jew nor Greek, slave nor free, male nor female, for you are all one in Christ Jesus"* (Galatians 3:28 BSB).
>
> *"The body is a unit, though it is made up of many parts; and though all its parts are many, they form one body. So it is with Christ. For we were all baptized by one Spirit into one body—whether Jews or Greeks, slave or free—and we were all given the one Spirit to drink"* (1 Corinthians 12:12-13).

Jesus spent time with everyone and never excluded others. He sat with those considered outsiders and befriended any who were interested. Jesus hung around the unpopular, the sick, and the sinners because he cared about them. We should do the same! We should try to live without judging others. We may feel that we are better than someone else because of things like our education, job, and skin color. However, the reality is that we are no better than anyone else. We all bleed the same, and all are deserving of respect as God's children. *"Rejoice with those who rejoice; mourn with those who mourn. Live in harmony with one another. Do not be proud, but be willing to associate with people of low position. Do not be conceited"* (Romans 12:15-18).

God the Father is conforming us into Jesus' image and wants us to follow his example. We know where he went, how he acted, and what he did. We get to read it and then follow his example in how we accept and treat others.

REFLECT

- What can you do to build more inclusive environments in all areas of your life?

Confessions of a Hot Mess - from MESS to MESSage

21
Blinded by Our Biases

Suppose a man comes into your meeting wearing a gold ring and fine clothes, and a poor man in filthy old clothes comes in. If you show special attention to the man wearing fine clothes and say, "Here's a good seat for you," but say to the poor man, "You stand there" or "Sit on the floor by my feet," have you not discriminated among yourselves and become judges with evil thoughts? (James 2:2-4).

I know we would like to think that we don't, but, as was mentioned in the last chapter, we all have biases. So, what is bias? It is defined as a prejudice in favor of or against a thing, person, or group compared with another, usually in a way that's considered to be unfair.

There are two types of biases:
- **Conscious bias** (also known as **explicit** bias) - Overt, negative behavior expressed through physical or verbal harassment or by more subtle means such as exclusion.

- **Unconscious bias** (also known as **implicit** bias) - Biases we don't realize we possess that influence a vast majority of our decisions.

So, how does this play out in our lives? We instinctively categorize people and things using easily observed criteria such as age, weight, race, and gender. But we also classify people according to other things such as educational level, disability, accent, social status, and job title, automatically assigning presumed traits to anyone we subconsciously put in those groups. Again, this saves us time and effort processing information about people, allowing us to spend more of our mental resources on other tasks. The clear disadvantage is that it can lead us to make assumptions about them and act based on biases we aren't even aware of.

What can we do to counteract the damage that unconscious biases can do?

<u>Take the time to identify biases that you have internalized</u>

There are tests—like Harvard's Implicit Association Test—that can help you figure out which of your perceptions are most likely to be governed by unconscious biases. Personally, I think that self-reflection is the best way to identify your potential areas of bias. You can do this by checking yourself when you catch yourself judging or making a quick assessment of someone else.

Once you identify your biases, educate yourself on different cultures and groups

Get to know some people from the groups or categories that you identify. Ask them questions and learn more about them to counteract the negative stereotypes that you may have. Remember that we are all God's children and worthy of respect and love.

Practice empathy

Putting yourself in others' shoes can help to decrease bias. This is easier once you have a better understanding of their culture or group.

Retrain your thoughts

Another way to overcome unconscious bias is to retrain the way you think by becoming aware of the tapes that run through your mind when encountering others. Once we are aware, we are better equipped to deal with situations in a more positive, bias-free manner.

Focus on the individual

Focus on what's distinctive about the individual, rather than the group they are part of.

God the Father is conforming us to Jesus' image and wants us to follow his example. We know where he went, how he acted, and what he did. We get to read it in the Bible and then follow his example in how we accept and treat others.

REFLECT

Take some time to reflect on biases that may be present in your life. Once you have identified your biases, take some proactive steps to overcome them.

_____
_____
_____
_____
_____
_____

22

Leading with Love

"But select capable men from all the people—men who fear God, trustworthy men who hate dishonest gain—appoint them as officials over thousands, hundreds, fifties and tens" (Exodus 18:21).

We have all had many different experiences with leadership–some great and probably, even more, not so great. Some leaders are self-serving and want to have all of the glory. Others micromanage or lead by intimidation. In my opinion, the best leaders lead with love. For much of my professional career, I have been involved with developing leaders. I continue to be amazed that many, once in a position of authority, forget the basics of treating others with respect in the manner they would like to be treated.

Do you think you're not a leader? Well, think again. We are all leaders in some form or fashion. It may be at work but also could be in the home or community. And we all have to lead ourselves!

I know that leading with love sounds kind of mushy. I'm not referring to warm and fuzzy feelings of love, but the kind of love that allows the person you are leading to be imperfectly human. This might involve the kindness of noticing that someone is having a bad day or feeling overwhelmed with the pressures of life. A leader that leads with love shows others that he/she cares about them and what's going on in their lives.

The key to leading with love is creating and nurturing a culture where people feel safe to be vulnerable. Vulnerability is one of those qualities we first look for in others but is often something that we are hesitant to show ourselves. Those that lead with love embrace their vulnerability, openly acknowledge their imperfections, and share how these imperfections allow them and others to learn and grow.

Leaders that lead with love don't just give positive feedback. They provide corrective feedback and expect others to learn from it. However, they will never make someone feel rejected for making a mistake. These leaders build a culture where tough love discussions can happen that build ever deeper connections with others. Psalm 32:8 says, *"I will instruct you and teach you in the way you should go; I will counsel you with my loving eye on you."*

A real leader is a servant of all. Let's take a look at Jesus' example.

> *You call me "Teacher" and "Lord," and rightly so, for that is what I am. Now that I, your Lord and Teacher, have washed your feet, you also should wash one another's feet. I have set you an example that you should do as I have done for you. I tell you the truth, no servant is greater than his master, nor is a messenger greater than the one who sent him. Now that you know these things, you will be blessed if you do them (John 13:13-17).*

Jesus was willing to wash the disciples' feet during their last meal. This wasn't some empty symbolic gesture but an example of true servant leadership. To follow Jesus' example, we should serve those that follow us. *"Do nothing out of selfish ambition or vain conceit, but in humility consider others better than yourselves" (Philippians 2:3).*

When it comes to leadership in organizations, poor leadership is terrible for the organization and demoralizing for the people under it. It needs to be dealt with quickly and strongly because if it's allowed to continue, it can undermine everything. *"When the righteous thrive, the people rejoice; when the wicked rule, the people groan" (Proverbs 29:2).*

As shepherds (or leaders), we must learn to be imitators of the Good Shepherd—following the example of Christ, leading by serving and guiding with love. Of course, we are human, and it's hard to do this all the time. But how much better would life be if we followed this example consistently as we lead in the home, community, and workplace? *"And David shepherded them with integrity of heart; with skillful hands he led them" (Psalm 78:72).*

REFLECT

- Where do you lead?
- What changes do you need to make to "lead with love?"

_____
_____
_____
_____
_____
_____
_____
_____

23
Are You Trustworthy?

Trust is the foundation of any strong relationship, whether in our personal lives or at work. Because God is trustworthy and because we are to emulate His character to the fullest possible extent, we, as believers, are also called to be trustworthy.

Ask yourself these questions: Am I trustworthy? Can my friends trust me to keep their confidence? Do I deliver on my promises? Can my boss trust me to do a thorough job? Can others trust me to be there for them when I say I will be?

If others feel that you are trustworthy, they feel that they can depend on you and that they can count on your discretion. They feel like they can let their guard down without fear of being taken advantage of or having their secrets broadcast all over town.

<u>Here are some behaviors that you should display to be trustworthy.</u>

- **Trust others:** If you want others to risk trusting you, you must take a risk on them first! Even though others will fail us at times, we can and should still trust people to varying degrees. We know that we can trust God, and He will never fail us, which makes us free to trust others.

- **Put others' interests before our own:** People are more likely to trust someone who they believe has their best interests at heart. As Christians, we are expected to care for the practical needs of others and put their interests before our own.

    Do nothing out of selfish ambition or vain conceit. Rather, in humility value others above yourselves, not looking to your own interests but each of you to the interests of others (Philippians 2:3-4).

- **Respect others:** Trustworthy people respect others. They believe that respect should be given to every human being. And they don't resort to behaviors such as intimidation or humiliation. *"So in everything, do to others what you would have them do to you, for this sums up the Law and the Prophets"* (Matthew 7:12).

- **Keep confidences:** Trustworthy people keep confidences. If someone tells them something privately, they do not share this information with others. *"Do not plot harm against your neighbor, who lives trustfully near you"* (Proverbs 3:29).

- **Don't gossip:** Trustworthy people don't gossip and talk negatively about others behind their backs. *"A gossip betrays a confidence, but a trustworthy person keeps a secret."* (Proverbs 11:13).

- **Apologize:** Trustworthy people admit and apologize for wrongs.

    "Confess your sins to each other and pray for each other so that you may be healed. The earnest prayer of a righteous person has great power and produces wonderful results" (James 5:16 NLT).

- **Be predictable:** Trustworthy people are predictable, and they don't let their emotions get the best of them. They are even-keeled and able to control their emotions and behavior. *"Like a snow-cooled drink at harvest time is a trustworthy messenger to the one who sends him; he refreshes the spirit of his master"* (Proverbs 25:13).

- **Keep your word:** Trustworthy people keep their word. Jesus said that we are to be speakers of truth and to speak this truth with love. *"Instead speaking the truth in love, we will grow to become in every respect the mature body of him who is the head, that is Christ"* (Ephesians 4:15).

- **Be open-minded:** Trustworthy people listen to others and keep an open mind. They are open to others' ideas and perspectives, instead of being judgmental and critical.

- **Be quick to listen to others:** Trustworthy people are good listeners. James 1:19 tells us to *"be quick to listen, slow to speak."*

I generally feel that I do a pretty good job of demonstrating the behaviors above. However, I can think of a recent circumstance where I fell short in keeping a confidence. I shared something with someone else that a friend had told me in confidence, thinking that the person I shared it with knew about it. I felt terrible and apologized profusely after it occurred. That said, we are all human and will likely fall short of being trustworthy on occasion. But we can do the best we can and pray that God will help to make us into a person that others can rely on.

REFLECT

- Do you think others see you as trustworthy?
- Looking at the information above, are there any areas that you need to work on?

24

Impeccable Integrity

"Whoever walks in integrity walks securely, but whoever takes crooked paths will be found out" (Proverbs 10:9).

I love this quote by Mark Twain: "If you tell the truth, you don't have to remember anything." There have been a few times in my life when I got caught up in a web of lies. Trying to date more than one guy at the same time is one example. We've all seen that movie when the guy or girl has two dates at the same place and is running back and forth, trying to conceal this from both individuals. It was never quite that crazy for me, but I did have a few instances when I was juggling more than one dude. I didn't want them to know about one another and couldn't quite keep track of what I had said to each one. And no surprise, this didn't turn out well.

We have all heard the term integrity and know that it's generally considered important. Integrity certainly includes honesty but goes beyond that. It connotes a deep commitment to do the right thing for the right reason, regardless of the circumstances—even when no one is watching. The word integrity evolved from a Latin adjective integer, meaning whole or complete. So, integrity is an inner sense of "wholeness" deriving from qualities such as honesty and consistent character.

I would have to give my husband a "ten out of ten" on integrity. He always tells the truth—at least as far as I can tell. I've never even heard him tell a little white lie. He is always the same, no matter what the environment or who we are with. He won't park in a spot if there is any bit of doubt about legality. He never breaks any rules. I don't know how his mama did it, but he has always been this way. We were sharing the worst things that we did in high school. I had a long list (and wasn't forthcoming about all of them). His worst thing was playing mini-golf until two o'clock in the morning with his parents' permission. How he got mixed up with a "hot mess," I'll never understand!

Our integrity is tested on a daily basis by a culture that has made falsehood and dishonesty a norm. This might involve cheating on a test, fudging a business expense, downloading music illegally from the internet, taking office supplies from work, or just telling little white lies. These sorts of actions can chip away at our integrity, one by one.

Consider these questions to self-assess your integrity:
- Do you portray yourself differently depending on who you are with?
- Do you admit your mistakes?
- Are you honest at all times?
- Can others depend on you to do what you say you'll do?

Scripture tells us many benefits of living with integrity:
- It can give us promotion the right way (Nehemiah 7)
- It grants favor and honor and opens the door for good things to come into our lives (Psalm 84:11)
- It can help us find contentment (Proverbs 19:1)
- It brings clarity and guidance to our lives (Proverbs 37:18)
- It helps us to be more like Jesus (Matthew 22:16)

David shed some light on integrity. In Psalm 26:1-3, he shared the ways he displayed his integrity.

> *Vindicate me, Lord; for I have led a blameless life: I have trusted in the Lord and have not faltered. Test me, Lord, and try me, examine my heart and my mind; for I have always been mindful of your unfailing love and have lived in reliance on your faithfulness.*

You can see here that the root of David's integrity is his relationship with God, as it should be for us.

How can you be sure that your integrity guides your actions? You will notice that there is quite a bit of overlap with the behaviors that you need to demonstrate to be trustworthy.

- **Keep your word:** If you say you are going to do something, then do it! If you say you are going to be somewhere, then be there! We probably all know people that we can't count on. Don't be one of those people!
- **Tell the truth:** Remember Mark Twain's quote! It's easier and the right thing to do. Even little white lies eat away at your integrity.
- **Don't gossip:** Keep confidences and don't talk about others behind

their backs. *"A gossip betrays a confidence, but a trustworthy person keeps a secret" (Proverbs 11:13).*

- **Work hard:** Colossians 3:23 says, *"Whatever you do, work at it with all your heart, as working for the Lord, not for human masters."* If you're a believer, your real boss is God, and whether or not anybody else sees your work, God does.

- **Act consistently:** A person of integrity doesn't act one way in church, another way at work, and another way in social settings. And a person of integrity treats the janitor with the same level of respect as the CEO.

God is never changing. He is faithful, trustworthy, true, and loyal. He can be counted on. He wants us to follow his example and live a life of integrity. *"The integrity of the upright guides them, but the unfaithful are destroyed by their duplicity" (Proverbs 11:3).*

REFLECT

- On a scale of 1 to 10, how would you rate yourself on "living a life of integrity?"

- If you are at a 10, you are definitely an enigma like my husband. If not, what could you do differently to increase the degree to which you demonstrate integrity in your life?

_____
_____
_____
_____
_____
_____
_____
_____
_____
_____
_____
_____
_____

RESPECT

"Show proper respect to everyone, love the family of believers, fear God, honor the emperor" (1 Peter 2:17).

Have you ever been treated with a lack of respect? I'm pretty sure that most of us have at one time or another. I certainly have at different times in my life. One fairly recent situation at work comes to mind. I had participated in a meeting where we had lunch in the conference room. Later that day, my boss flagged me down and instructed me to move the tea jug out of the room. He was standing right beside it. Really? And I knew for sure that he would have never done that if I had been male. And this was not the first time I felt disrespected by him. Needless to say, I no longer work there.

So, why do we need to respect others? Remember the golden rule.

- *"Do to others as you would have them do to you"* (Luke 6:31).
- *"So in everything, do to others what you would have them do to you, for this sums up the Law and the Prophets"* (Matthew 7:12).

Here are some examples of ways that we can show respect to others:
- Treat them with courtesy and kindness
- Encourage them to share their opinions
- Listen to them without speaking over or interrupting them
- Don't insult, name-call, disparage or belittle them
- Be inclusive

We know that others have faults, and there may be times when we need to discuss problems, yet the Bible tells us that we need to maintain an attitude of respect for everybody.

Here are some reasons why God expects us to respect others:

They are made in the image of God

The Bible says, *"for in the image of God has God made mankind"* (Genesis 9:6b). Whether or not someone is a Christian, honor him or her as God's creation.

They are children of God

In addition, we should respect others as children of God and realize that God loves them as such. We should never dishonor someone God loves.

We should love our neighbors as ourselves

The Bible instructs us to *"love your neighbor as yourself"* (Mark 12:30-31). You can't love your neighbor and not show them respect!

You may feel certain people don't deserve your respect, but you should show them respect because God said to. The Bible gives us an example with respect to marital relationships.

> *"However, each one of you also must love his wife as he loves himself, and the wife must respect her husband"* (Ephesians 5:33).

> *"Husbands, in the same way, be considerate as you live with your wives, and treat them with respect..."* (1 Peter 3:7). I stopped there because it goes on to say the wife is the weaker partner. I still have some work to do to get there!

The same principle applies to other relationships. Peter wrote that we should show respect to everyone and honor the king, even though the king in those days was an evil person. (1 Peter 2:17)

So, go forth and show everyone respect!

REFLECT

- Do you consistently show respect to everyone, whether you feel they deserve it or not?
- If not, what will you do to ensure that you are!

_____
_____
_____
_____
_____

Leslie Speas

Section 3:

Managing Your Mind

LESLIE SPEAS

26
Taming My Crazy Mind

Does anyone else feel like they have a crazy mind? Mine is constantly going and often to places where it isn't necessarily healthy for it to go. My husband and I were hiking one day, and I asked him what he was thinking about. He replied, "I'm thinking about where I am going to put my pole next." I had already done a review of the last few years, worried about my kids' futures, and planned our next vacation, and we were only twenty minutes in. What I would give to have a mind like his! I often feel like my mind is in constant turmoil. I don't know about you, but I really struggle to make my mind mind!

Proverbs 4:23 (NCV) says, *"Be careful what you think because your thoughts run your life."* Until I started reading about and researching the topic, I didn't realize that it was possible to control what you think about. In 2 Corinthians 10:3-5, we are instructed to take our thoughts captive:

> *For though we live in the world, we do not wage war as the world does. The weapons we fight with are not the weapons of the world. On the contrary, they have divine power to diminish strongholds. We demolish arguments and every pretension that sets itself up against the knowledge of God, and we take captive every thought to make it obedient to Christ.*

Here are a few things that I've done to try to tame my crazy mind with some success, so I thought I'd share. I definitely plan to keep at it!

Identify the root of the thought

When you have a negative thought, try to identify the root cause. Ask yourself, "Where did it come from?" and "Is there an underlying issue or theme?" If you can gain clarity on these things, you can begin to gain control of your thought life.

Recognize and reject Satan's lies

Satan tempts and troubles us by putting ideas and thoughts in our minds, preying on our struggles and past hurts. Recognize and reject his lies and replace them with God's truth (look for passages to support His truth. If I have an ungodly thought, I try to redirect myself and say, "Get away, Satan," and ask God for the strength to help me overcome. Helpful tip - You may want to say "Get away, Satan" to yourself, or you might get some unwanted attention.

Focus on the good things/blessings around you

This includes having eyes to see, ears to hear, family, friends, a place to live, nature, and so many more things. Keeping a gratitude journal and writing down three things that you are thankful for each day can be helpful.

Memorize Scripture

Here are a few Scriptures that have helped me:

* *"Set your mind on things above, not on earthly things"* (Colossians 3:2).

* *"Finally, brothers, whatever is true, whatever is noble, whatever is right, whatever is pure, whatever is lovely, whatever is admirable – if anything is excellent or praiseworthy – think about such things. Whatever you have learned or received or heard from me or seen in me—put it into practice. And the God of peace will be with you"* (Philippians 4:8-9).

Ensure that you are allowing time to nurture your soul.

This includes reading the Bible, prayer, exercise, solitude, and rest.

These are all good practices to train and transform our hearts and minds. For those who suffer from crazy minds like mine, I hope this is helpful. Pray for me, and I'll pray for you as well that we can *"set our minds on things above."*

REFLECT

* Think about what you think about. Begin to take your thoughts captive and redirect them to more positive thoughts.

_____
_____
_____
_____
_____
_____
_____

27

I Am Enough!

"How great is the love the Father has lavished on us, that we should be called children of God! And that is what we are!" (1 John 3:1).

We all have narratives in our minds that guide our thoughts and actions. These are stories that we frequently tell ourselves. These narratives may be based on how we grew up, our experiences, and our culture. What bad news do you tell yourself every day?

One of the narratives that has guided my life is "I'm not good enough." This narrative goes through my head frequently and negatively impacts my life. I think part of this stems from my parents' divorce where, although it didn't have anything to do with me, I believed at some level that I was partially at fault and that I wasn't worth staying for. I also felt that I didn't please my father with my college or career choice and generally felt like a disappointment.

Later, I was in a verbally abusive relationship, which confirmed in my mind that I wasn't good enough. Until I read a few books on the subject, I had never really thought about the story I was telling myself. Some examples of how this narrative has plagued me over the years and may be plaguing some of you are below:

- I'm not enough!
- I'm not strong enough.
- I'm not smart enough.
- I'm not brave enough.
- I'm not talented enough.
- I'm not enough of a good mother/good spouse/good friend/good employee.
- I'm not thin enough.
- I'm not pretty enough.

So many other people say or do unkind things to us in this world. We should be kind and speak to ourselves as we would a friend! As Proverbs 18:21 says, *"The tongue has the power of life or death."* And that is whether we are using it to talk to ourselves or others!

It has helped me to read scripture that confirms how God sees me—and this is how He sees you too:

- I am deeply and completely loved (Romans 8:38-39)
- I am fearfully and wonderfully made (Psalm 139:14)
- I am holy and dearly loved (Colossians 3:12)
- I am free from condemnation (Romans 8:1)
- I am totally and completely forgiven (1 John 2:12)
- I mean the world to Him (John 3:16)
- He thinks I am beautiful right now (Song of Solomon 4:1)
- When God sees me, He sees the righteousness of Jesus (2 Corinthians 5:21)

I'm sure that some of you also struggle with feeling like you aren't good enough. When you recognize this false belief, reject it, and replace it with these truths.

In *Enough: Silencing the Lies That Steal Your Confidence*, Sharon Jaynes suggests trying to recognize I AM NOT thoughts and speech and switch them with I AM. When you say, "I AM NOT smart enough," mentally change this to "I AM" smart enough." Sharon suggests "spotting the nots" in your life, swatting them out of your mind, and replacing them with the truth.

God made us for a purpose, and that includes our talents, bodies, quirks, weaknesses, and passions. You are the only one alive who was or ever will be you. I am trying to grow in believing that I am completely loved in the moment and that God isn't waiting for me to get my act together for me to be worthy. He knows everything about me and loves me anyway. We are enough because of Jesus' presence and power in us.

Friends, you are loved. You do enough. You are enough.

REFLECT

- What are the lies that you tell yourself?
- What can you do to help overcome these narratives and "spot the nots"?

28
Comparison - The Thief of Joy

"Each one should test his own actions. Then he can take pride in himself, without comparing himself to somebody else..." (Galatians 6:4).

Often when I feel like I have gotten to a good place in my life, along comes someone that seems like they have it much better in comparison. I know that I personally have the tendency to make comparisons, and I'm pretty sure that I'm not alone in that. Comparing ourselves to others steals our peace and joy!

We may perceive that others have more money, a better house, a better job, more well-behaved or successful kids, which makes us feel bad about ourselves. Never has this been more prevalent than with the emergence of social media, where the Joneses are in our face all the time. It just takes a scroll to see an update that makes us feel envious or like our life pales in comparison to others. I know that I feel pangs of jealousy when I see pictures of fabulous vacations, families that seem to have it all together, or a younger friend looking fabulous in her bikini.

We compare our circumstances or abilities to someone else's and come to this conclusion: I could never do it like she does it. And you know what? We were never meant to! God doesn't need two people who are just alike. He has uniquely and precisely created you and me with specific gifts and talents to do what He's called us to do. Who are we to question His plan for us? Reflect on what it says in Ephesians 2:10 (BSB): *"For we are God's workmanship, created in Christ Jesus to do his good works, which God prepared in advance for us to do."*

We have great value in God's eyes, so why do we constantly make these comparisons? It is so easy to think that if we had more or knew more, we'd be happy. However, even people who "have it all" still struggle with feelings of insecurity. The Bible opens with the story of Eve, a woman who had everything, but it wasn't enough for her. She wanted more and was tempted to try to get it.

What can we do to stop comparing ourselves to others?

<u>*Become aware of and avoid your triggers*</u>

Start noticing the triggers that cause you to play the comparison game. Social media is a big one for most of us. Are there other activities or circumstances that frequently make you feel discontent about your life? Identify those and try to avoid them.

Realize that other people's "outer appearance" can't be compared to your "insides"

More often than not, you can't use a person's outward appearance to judge the reality of their life. People carefully craft their social media and public personas. I know that I've personally been shocked when that "perfect couple" announced they were splitting up. Or, in the worst possible scenario, someone who seems to have it all together commits suicide.

Count your blessings

Think about what you have and are already blessed with. Try to focus on what you have, not what you don't. Think about how fortunate you are to have the people and things that are in your life.

Focus on the Lord

Focus on Him when you are tempted to compare yourself with others. David was given armor that was too large for him when he was going to fight Goliath. David didn't go searching for different armor. Instead, he focused on God's character. He knew that God had helped him in the past and would continue to as he faced Goliath. We need to constantly remind ourselves of His faithfulness. We can be content as long as we keep our eyes focused on God, the only one worth looking at. We have much greater things to do than size ourselves up or measure our kids against the neighbors'.

I loved this poem that I came across on the internet:

> *The stick I made for measuring*
> *I used most every day.*
> *It helped me to compare myself*
> *with others on my way.*
> *I watched all those behind me,*
> *or further down the road,*
> *and I would readjust my pace*
> *or lighten up my load.*
> *The only real drawback*
> *with how I ran my race*
> *I was watching everything around,*
> *except my Savior's face.*
>
>   Anne Peterson, freelance author and poet

It's time we stop comparing ourselves to others. God made you to be you, and he thinks you're magnificent. Take courage in that amazing thought—I am.

REFLECT

- Is comparison an issue that you struggle with frequently?
- If so, what triggers you to compare yourself to others?
- What are some things that you will do to try to overcome the tendency to compare?

29

Do Not Conform to the Standards of This World

"Do not conform to the pattern of this world, but be transformed by the renewing of your mind. Then you will be able to test and approve what God's will is —his good, pleasing and perfect will" (Romans 12:2).

Many of us operate under a false narrative that happiness comes from following the principles of this world. This usually means achievement, material possessions, money, sex, and power. The things that the world values are not what God values. God looks for obedience and faithfulness. He looks for humility instead of pride. In Romans 12:2, we are instructed not to conform to the standards of this world.

Many of us identify with what we do for a living and feel that this makes us a success in life. Our work shouldn't be the source of our identity, but an extension of our identity in Christ. What we do for a living doesn't make us better than others. Although certain occupations carry more power and prestige in this world than others, that is not what is important to God.

Wealth and possessions can easily numb us to our need for God and result in us overlooking the needs of others. But today's possessions will become tomorrow's load to dump. Now, friends, I love me some shopping, especially for clothes and shoes, and often struggle with a focus on possessions. I have all that I need but want more! Cutting down on personal shopping and either saving those funds or redirecting them to those in need is one of my goals this year. There I said it! Help me be accountable. I need to remember that earthly treasures are temporary while heavenly treasures are eternal.

Consider these verses from Scripture as further education around this topic:

- *"No one can serve two masters. Either he will hate the one and love the other, or he will be devoted to the one and despise the other. You cannot serve both God and Money" (Matthew 6:24).*

- *"Do not store up for yourself treasures on earth, where moth and rust destroy, and where thieves break in and steal. But store up for yourself treasures in heaven, where moth and rust do not destroy, and where thieves do not break in and steal. For where your* treasure is, there your heart will be also" (Matthew 6:19-21 BSB).

- "Those who trust in their riches will fall, but the righteous will thrive like a green leaf" (Proverbs 11:28).

- "One pretends to be rich, yet has nothing; another pretends to be poor, yet has great wealth" (Proverbs 13:7 ESV).

- "Believers in humble circumstances ought to take pride in their high position. But the rich should take pride in their humiliation—since they will pass away like a wild flower" (James 1:9-10).

We should live to create an eternal legacy, not an earthy one. In *The Purpose Driven Life*, Rick Warren says:

> When you believe that there is more to life than here and now, you realize that life is preparation for eternity. When you live in the light of eternity, your values change. You place a higher premium on relationships and character instead of fame or wealth or achievements.

Here are a few verses that further emphasize this point:

- "Friends, this world is not your home, so don't make yourselves cozy in it. Don't indulge your ego at the expense of your soul" (1 Corinthians 4:2 MSG).

- "So we fix our eyes not on what is seen, but on what is unseen, since what is seen is temporary, but what is unseen is eternal" (Luke 12:48).

We are never completely happy in this world because we aren't supposed to be. We all have a God-shaped hole that we may try to fill with people, possessions, or power, but these things will not ultimately make us happy. Lasting joy can be found only by knowing Jesus Christ.

I was humbled researching this topic because I am often focused on the things that the world values—primarily achievement and materialism. I am going to meditate on these verses and ask God to change me. If this is a struggle for you, you may want to consider doing the same.

REFLECT

- What worldly things or possessions do you tend to focus on?

- What will you do to help overcome this tendency?

Confessions of a Hot Mess- from MESS to MESSage

30

Grace Not Works

"Amazing Grace" is one of my favorite hymns – and certainly one of the most well-known hymns of all time. Here are some of its beautiful words:

> Amazing grace—how sweet the sound—
> That saved a wretch like me!
> I once was lost but now am found,
> Was blind but now I see.

I used to operate under the false narrative that I had to somehow earn God's favor. If I did something that I felt was wrong or I wasn't focused on my relationship with Him, I was afraid that He would do something bad in my life to get my attention. I honestly fretted over this and felt like I needed to get my act together, or it would be hell to pay--oops, maybe an inappropriate play on words. But you get my drift. Sounds kind of silly, doesn't it? We are human and will always screw up. We will never be good enough or do good enough to earn God's favor.

My mindset was mired in legalism, which promotes the earning and keeping of God's love based upon what you do or do not do. It's not surprising that we feel compelled to earn salvation based on works as acceptance in this world is typically performance-based. After all, getting salvation through grace is too good to be true, isn't it? Ephesians 28:8-9 (ESV) says, *"For by grace you have been saved through faith. And this is not your own doing; it is the gift of God, not a result of works, so that no one may boast."*

What exactly is grace? There are many definitions of grace, but one that I especially like is "the freely given, unmerited favor and love of God." Grace is essentially undeserved favor; it is God's blessing on the unworthy.

There is an acronym that is sometimes used for grace which I thought was pretty cool:

> **G**od's
> **R**iches
> **A**t
> **C**hrist's
> **E**xpense

The Bible says that we are saved by grace. This grace is expressed by God's forgiveness of our sins, His blessings in this life, and the promise of unencumbered fellowship with Him for eternity. Wow, the gift of grace truly is amazing!

We have maintained that we cannot work our way to heaven by our good works, but we should have good works, shouldn't we? If Jesus is in our hearts, we will be compelled to do good works and help others. *"In the same way, let your light shine before others, that they may see your good deeds and glorify your Father in heaven"* (Matthew 5:16).

In conclusion, here are a few more Scriptures that tell us more about God's amazing grace:

- *"From the fullness of His grace we have all received one blessing after another"* (John 1:16).

- *"...to the praise of his glorious grace, which he has freely given us in the One he loves"* (Ephesians 1:6).

REFLECT

- Take a few moments to reflect on the gift of grace that God has given us. Isn't it amazing?

___
___
___
___
___
___
___
___
___
___
___
___
___
___
___
___

31

Let Go and Let God

"…God, the blessed and only ruler, the King of kings and the Lord of lords" (1 Timothy 6:15.

Does anyone else like the feeling of being in control? I love to have my plans and feel like I have control over how things will go. It's too bad that others are not following my plan because their lives—and mine—would be so much better!

I am having a very difficult time relinquishing the need to control my young adult children. For some reason, they are not following my plan for their lives. Shocking, I know! When they were younger, I felt like I had some control over what they did, what they wore, who they hung out with, etc. Now, I don't even have the illusion of control. They are on the cusp of making so many decisions that will impact their lives long-term—what career to choose, how they take care of their health, who to have a relationship with or marry, to name a few—and they rarely listen to me anymore! I also know that I'm way too concerned about appearances and need to let it go, but rainbow hair, nose piercings, and Birkenstocks with socks and sweatpants were not a part of my plan for them.

Proverbs 19:21 says, *"Many are the plans in a person's heart, but it is the Lord's purpose that prevails."* I have come to realize that I'm rarely, if ever, in control of what happens. It's all God. I may have control over my actions, attitude, and responses, but that's about it. Even knowing this, when something happens that concerns me, I still get in there and try to set things straight. I guess this means that I secretly still think that I'm in control and don't trust God to handle it. I know that the destinies of my children and all the other things that I try to control are better off in God's hands, not in my faltering, grabby ones. I have prayed and prayed but still haven't been successful in surrendering.

How can we let go and let God? Below are some suggestions:

<u>Surrender to God</u>

First, we have to confess and surrender our need for control. God asks us to trust him with what we can't see. Second Corinthians 5:7 (BSB) tells us to *"walk by faith, not by sight."* One article I read suggested taking a piece of paper and writing down the things you are holding onto tightly. It then said to lay the pieces of paper on the floor and imagine you are laying them at the feet of the Father.

Meditate on Truths About Him

Meditating on truths about God can help us to overcome our need for control. Some of the scripture in this section may be helpful to read and meditate on. When you have a controlling thought, say, *"Not my will, but yours be done!"*

Don't Doubt

God knows what you need and when you need it. Trust Him to take care of it for you. When we let God drive our lives and trust that He knows best, we can rest and stop striving. Think about and jot down in your journal difficult situations that God has helped you through. When you need a reminder, read the journal.

God assures us that *"for those who love God all things work together for good" (Romans 8:28 ESV).* Even when He seems to be taking us down a different path than we had planned to take, He will work it for good.

In conclusion, control (or lack of it) continues to be a big struggle for me. I will continue to pray about and try to accept that God is weaving together a far happier ending than anything I can do. I am going to pray and meditate over Psalm 31:3-5 whenever I need a reminder: *"Since you are my rock and my fortress, for the sake of your name lead and guide me. Free me from the trap that is set for me, for you are my refuge. Into your hands I commit my spirit, redeem me, O Lord, the God of truth."*

REFLECT

- Do you struggle with trying to control things in your life? If so, in what areas?
- What are some situations that God has helped you through that can serve as a reminder of his love and power in your life?
- What actions will you take to "let go and let God?"

_____
_____
_____
_____
_____
_____
_____

32

Facing Your Fears

"So do not fear, for I am with you; do not be dismayed, for I am your God. I will strengthen you and help you; I will uphold you with my righteous right hand" (Isaiah 41:10).

What are your fears? Here's just a few of mine: harm coming to a loved one, rejection, debilitating illness, financial ruin, indecent exposure in public, and failure. Also, spiders, snakes, frogs, lizards, and most bugs (ladybugs are okay, I guess).

Fear is defined as "a distressing emotion aroused by an impending pain, danger, evil, etc., or the illusion of such." To best understand fear, it's important to distinguish between fear and anxiety. They often occur together, but these terms are not interchangeable. Fear comes from a known or understood threat, whereas anxiety comes from an unknown, expected, or poorly defined threat.

There are two types of fear–healthy and unhealthy. The first kind protects us from harm and is tied to our fight-or-flight reflex. Healthy fear also promotes reverence and respect for God. The second type of fear includes irrational fears which come from Satan and are designed to make us miserable and destroy our lives.

I recently discovered Michelle Poler, a young woman who had lived her life paralyzed by fear. She launched a Fear Challenge where she faced a fear each day for 100 days and has inspired many across the globe to try to overcome their fears. She sky-dived, zip-lined, braved roller-coasters, held a tarantula, rode a bull, and much more. You may not want to go to these lengths, but here are some things that may help you fight your fears.

<u>Name Your Fears</u>

What are some of your unhealthy or irrational fears? Sometimes merely naming your fears helps give you the awareness and strength to deal with them.

<u>Read the Word of God</u>

The greatest weapon against fear is the Word of God. The Bible tells us not to fear over two hundred times. Here are some Bible verses that I found inspiring for overcoming fear.

- "I sought the Lord, and he answered me; he delivered me from all my fears" (Psalm 34:4).

- "All your children will be taught by the Lord, and great shall be their peace. In righteousness you will be established: Tyranny will be far from you; you will have nothing to fear. Terror will be far removed; it will not come near you" (Isaiah 54:13-14).

- "...God has said, 'Never will I leave you; never will I forsake you.' So we may say with confidence: 'The Lord is my helper; I will not be afraid. What can mere mortals do to me?" (Hebrews 13:5-6).

Face Your Fears

What if we actually faced our fears and did things we thought we'd never do?

- If you are afraid of public speaking, do it anyway!
- If you are afraid of air travel, take a flight!
- If you are afraid of taking on a project because you might fail, take it on!

Stop saying that you can't or won't and go after the "I can do it because my God is able!" I can tell you for sure that I will not be holding a snake or a spider— or singing in public. However, I like the idea of facing my fears and may work towards a mini-Fear Challenge. One hundred days might be a bit much for me.

Trust in God

Trusting in God is our ultimate remedy for fear. Yet, that sometimes seems easier said than done. He tells us that perfect love casts out fear and that He is love.

> "There is no fear in love. But perfect love drives out fear because fear has to do with punishment. The one who fears is not made perfect in love" (1 John 4:18).

Here is an exercise that may help to solidify your trust in God. Try writing out a list of things that you have irrational fears about. Then present each of them to God. After giving them all to God, rip up your list—or burn it if you want to be really dramatic.

You can also read the following Scriptures when you need reminders to trust God:

- *"When I am afraid, I put my trust in you"* (Psalm 56:3 BSB).

- *"The Lord is with me; I will not be afraid. What can mere mortals do to me? The Lord is with me; he is my helper"* (Psalm 118:6-7).

Focus on the Positive

We are wired to focus on the negative. It's called the negativity response. In Philippians, Paul tells believers what they should focus on. He doesn't mention fear, terrorism, or failure.

> *Finally, brothers and sisters, whatever is true, whatever is noble, whatever is right, whatever is pure, whatever is lovely, whatever is admirable—if anything is excellent or praiseworthy—think about such things. Whatever you have learned or received or heard from me, or seen in me—put it into practice. And the God of peace will be with you (Philippians 4:8-9).*

We will end with one of my favorite Scriptures: *"Even though I walk through the darkest valley, I will fear no evil, for you are with me; your rod and your staff, they comfort me"* (Psalm 23:4).

REFLECT

- What are some of your unhealthy or irrational fears?

- What will you do to try to overcome these fears?

_____
_____
_____
_____
_____
_____
_____
_____
_____
_____
_____
_____
_____

33
Attacking Anxiety

As was shared in the last chapter, there is a difference between fear and anxiety. Fear comes from a known or understood threat, whereas anxiety comes from an unknown, expected, or poorly defined threat. Experiencing occasional anxiety is a normal part of life. However, people who suffer from excessive anxiety or anxiety disorders often have intense, frequent, and persistent anxiety and fear about everyday situations.

Chances are that you or someone you are close to struggles with anxiety. Anxiety disorders in the U.S. are the number one mental health problem among women and are second to only alcohol and drug abuse among men. Interestingly enough, all four of our grown kids are having regular struggles with anxiety. "You're welcome," kids, for putting this out there. And my husband, who appears to be the most laid-back dude around, has anxiety attacks from time to time.

In his book *Anxious for Nothing*, Max Lucado describes anxiety as a low-grade fear. An edginess, a dread. A cold wind that won't stop howling. He says anxiety is a meteor shower of what-ifs. Until this last year, I had only had one full-on anxiety attack one time, complete with breathing in a paper bag. This was brought on by feelings of anxiety related to the end of my first marriage. With the pandemic and my mother's unexpected death recently, I have had several anxiety attacks over the last few months, but hopefully am coming out the other side.

I've certainly experienced a fair amount of generalized anxiety from time to time during my life. I've been anxious about what-ifs such as terrorist attacks, losing my job, my kids having a wreck, and just about everything else at some point. I've even been anxious about being anxious because Christians are supposed to be "anxious for nothing," right? In his book, Max Lucado points out that anxiety is not a sin: it is an emotion. However, anxiety can lead to sinful behavior. If we don't watch ourselves, we may try to deal with it by doing things like drinking too much, doing drugs, getting angry, or binging on food.

Philippians 4:6-7 tells us,

> *Do not be anxious about anything, but in every situation, by prayer and petition, with thanksgiving, present your requests to God. And*

the peace of God, which transcends all understanding, will guard your hearts and your minds in Christ Jesus.

Our instructions continue by telling us to focus on what is true, noble, right, pure, lovely, admirable, excellent, or praiseworthy (Philippians 4:8-9).

If you struggle with anxiety, intentional stress management practices can be helpful. These practices include deep breathing, prayer, meditation, yoga, exercise, and taking time for yourself. I will tell you that, personally, yoga changed my life. I have been into fitness for many years. I used to think yoga was for sissies and didn't totally understand it. It took me some time, but the stretching, breathing, and mindfulness bring me relief, comfort and slows my mind down (if even for a short time). Doing cardio or weight training also helps me release some of my pent-up stress and anxiety. We will talk more about stress management in a later chapter.

As I said before, I am a firm believer that counseling can be helpful and that there is no shame in seeking some outside assistance. I have participated in counseling to deal with several difficult circumstances in my life. It made a huge positive impact!

If someone you love struggles with chronic anxiety, you can help by noticing, caring, and being available to help. This could involve picking up their kids, providing a meal, or lending a caring ear. A little kindness and compassion will go a long way to help them through.

As Christians, we have God's promises that He will take care of us, love us, and protect us. We realize that He is in control of all things. And we know that He is working things together for the good of those who love Him. I'm quite far from being "anxious for nothing," but I'm learning to focus more on Him and His promises and not on my fear.

REFLECT

* Do you experience issues with anxiety in your life? What are some things that you could do to help you positively deal with this?

* Who in your life struggles with anxiety? What could you do to help them?

_____
_____
_____
_____

34

Worry Woman

"Who of you by worrying can add a single hour to his life?" (Matthew 6:27 BSB).

If I were a superhero, I would likely be Worry Woman as I think worry is my superpower. I am pretty darn good at it. Worry is anxiety's BFF. Worry occurs in our minds and is usually specific, whereas anxiety is felt in our bodies and tends to be more diffused. I have certainly spent (or should I say wasted) a lot of my life worrying about everything, including finances, my children, my job, and the future. I guess you could call me a worrywart, but I get it honest. My mother could have won an Olympic medal for worrying.

Here's a typical day for me:

- I wake up a little later than usual and worry about whether I will get all my morning activities done and get to work on time.
- I look in the mirror and worry about the extra gray hairs and wrinkles that have popped up. Do I need to dye my hair again? Is Botox an option?
- I don't have time for breakfast, so I grab a pop tart and then worry about the calories and sugar.
- I scroll through Facebook and see how amazing my friends' kids are and worry that I haven't been a good mom.
- I feel a pain in my back and worry that I'm going to have to have surgery.
- I watch the news and worry about global warming and the economy.

Has any good ever come from worry? I haven't seen any evidence of it. Worrying wastes precious time and robs us of the ability to enjoy our lives. It's choosing to dwell on and to think about the worst-case scenario, which, more than likely, will never come to pass.

Worry, in essence, is the sin of distrusting the promises and the power of God. We believe God can redeem us, defeat Satan, and give us eternal life, but we don't think He can get us through the week. Kind of ironic, isn't it? This shows a serious lack of faith. Also, when we worry, we torment ourselves, doing Satan's job for him!

In Matthew 6:25, Jesus says, *"Do not worry about your life, what you will eat or drink; or about your body, what you will wear. Is not life more than food, and the body more than clothes?"*

I know I spend a lot of time worrying about eating, drinking, and what I'm going to wear. How much more productive would it be to focus this energy on doing something else?

God wants so much more for us than to walk through life full of worry. To begin to overcome it, we must humbly admit that we can't do life in our own strength and turn over our problems to Him. Here are a few Scriptures to help us in this area:

* *"'Come to me, all you who labor and are heavy laden, and I will give you rest. Take my yoke upon you, and learn from me, for I am gentle and lowly in heart, and you will find rest for your souls. For my yoke is easy and my burden is light"* (Matthew 11:28-30 ESV).

* *"Cast all of your anxiety on him because he cares for you"* (1 Peter 5:7).

God gives you the wonderful gift of life today so try to live in the light and full joy of the day. Try not to push yourself into the future and give up the day's joy over an anticipated tomorrow that may likely never happen.

REFLECT

* What do you worry about?

* What will you do to try to overcome the tendency to worry and trust God more?

_____
_____
_____
_____
_____
_____
_____

35

Stress Less

".. keep my eyes always on the LORD. With him at my right hand, I will not be shaken" (Psalm 16:8).

Has anyone ever taken the assessment where you get a rating of your stress level based on what is going on in your life? I remember doing this assessment when I had a ton of significant changes in my life—including a new marriage, blending families, a new job, and a house under construction. My score was through the roof. I don't recommend doing all these things at one time! And this year hasn't exactly been a walk in the park with the loss of my mom, multiple moves for the kids, a broken foot, and COVID 2.0.

Stress is defined as a feeling that people have when overloaded and struggling to cope with demands. These demands can be related to finances, work, relationships, or children. Anything that poses a real or perceived threat to our well-being can cause stress. Stress isn't always bad. It is, in fact, essential to survival. The fight-or-flight mechanism alerts us when and how to respond to danger. However, if this mechanism is triggered too easily, or when there are too many stressors at one time, it can undermine a person's mental and physical health and become harmful.

Stress can affect your body, your emotions, and your behavior. Being able to recognize common stress symptoms can help you manage them. Here are common stress symptoms from the Mayo Clinic:

- **Impact of stress on your body.** Headaches, fatigue, lack of sleep, muscle tension or pain, upset stomach, chest pains.

- **Impact of stress on your thoughts and emotions.** Anxiety, restlessness, lack of motivation, feeling overwhelmed, anger.

- **Impact of stress on your behavior.** Overeating or undereating, use of drugs and alcohol, tobacco use, angry outbursts, social withdrawal.

As you can see, stress can take a serious toll on our well-being. Most importantly, it derails our relationship with God and distracts us, which provides inroads for Satan to work in our lives.

Most of us are aware of common ways to manage our stress, such as exercise, yoga, and meditation. These are all good techniques, but let's look at some biblical ways to deal with stress.

Pray through stress

This requires us to focus on God and shifts our attention from our earthly issues.

Ask for help

Stress can often be a signal that we have too much on our plates. Ask for help from family, friends, coworkers, or seek professional help.

Seek Community

The body of Christ is meant to strengthen us when we're weak, help us in times of need, and support us during difficult times. Stay connected with people who care about you.

Read God's Word

Meditate on scripture and invite the Holy Spirit to work in your heart.

Lighten your load

Examine what's on your plate. Too much prolonged stress may mean it is time to start saying no and lightening your load.

The only way we can consistently and successfully deal with stress is with Jesus Christ. We must believe in Him. We must trust Him and obey Him. We must remember that His ways are always best for us.

REFLECT

- What is creating stress in your life?
- Over the next few weeks, try some of the biblical ways suggested to deal with your stress.

_____
_____
_____
_____
_____
_____
_____

36

Anger Management

"Whoever is slow to anger has great understanding, but he who has a hasty temper exalts folly" (Proverbs 14:29 ESV).

Anger is commonly defined as "a strong feeling of annoyance, displeasure, or hostility." The Mayo Clinic says that anger is a natural response to a perceived threat against our well-being or position. This response causes the body to release adrenaline, muscles to tighten, and heart rate and blood pressure to increase. As humans, we are going to get angry sometimes; it's just part of life. Although feeling anger sometimes is normal, we should not cling to these feelings and act out or hold grudges.

So, what makes you angry? I occasionally get road rage. And I certainly get angry if someone is ugly to my kids or loved ones. And certain people (won't mention names here) tend to push my buttons to the point that I lose my cool at times. And bad customer service can turn me into a "Karen" (sorry to my friends named Karen). I'm sure none of you have had this problem, but I used to feel like I was doing everything around the house and that I wasn't valued. I would eventually erupt on my family members. I have chilled in my older age and don't tend to grow angry as quickly as I used to.

The Bible teaches that uncontrolled anger is harmful, both to the person who harbors it and to those around him or her (Proverbs 29:22). Further, the Bible says that those who continue to have "fits of anger" will not inherit God's kingdom (Galatians 5:19-21). Remember Cain? Cain "grew hot with anger" when God rejected his sacrifice. Cain's anger then festered to the point that he murdered his brother (Genesis 4:3-8).

James 1:19 (NASB) says, *"...let everyone be quick to hear, slow to speak and slow to anger."* He isn't necessarily saying that anger is wrong but is telling us not to be quick-tempered. Paul told the Ephesians pretty much the same thing: *"Be angry, and yet do not sin; do not let the sun go down on your anger..." (Ephesians 4:26 NASB).* I can think of lots of times when the sun went down on my anger. I have slept on the very corner of the bed, trying my best not to touch my husband because I was angry. Not so much this husband, but definitely the first one.

Here are a few methods of controlling your anger so it doesn't get the best of you.

Just say no

When you feel yourself getting upset, immediately say "No!" to those thoughts and feelings. Instead of letting the anger control you, take some deep breaths, and say a prayer.

Take a break

Proverbs 17:14 (NWT) says, *"Before the quarrel breaks out, take your leave."* Although you should try to settle differences quickly, sometimes you may need to take a break and cool down before addressing the situation with the other person(s).

Get the facts

Proverbs 19:11 (NWT) says, *"the insight of a man certainly slows down his anger."* Gather all the facts and get all sides of the story before jumping to conclusions.

Give others a little grace

Remember that most of us are going through difficulties in our lives. Recognize that there are probably underlying reasons that others may be behaving badly and give them some grace.

Pray for a peaceful mind

Through prayer, we can experience *"the peace of God, which transcends all understanding"* (Philippians 4:7).

> *"He who is slow to anger is better than the mighty"* (Proverbs 16:32 NKJV).

REFLECT

- What makes you angry?
- What can you do to manage your anger better?

_____
_____
_____
_____

37

Marvelous Mindfulness

"Test me, Lord, and try me, examine my heart and my mind; for I have always been mindful of your unfailing love and have lived in reliance on your faithfulness" (Psalm 26:2-3).

Have you ever had the experience of driving somewhere and not recalling how you got there? Or going to an event and not remembering the details afterward? Or even being with a family member or friend and not remembering much about the interaction?

In today's world, we have an overabundance of distractions and stimuli coming at us from different directions. We live busy lives, overcrowded with work, caring for others, school, volunteering, church, and more. Cell phones and social media have further complicated our lives. It's no wonder our minds wander! But when they do, we can miss a lot. The fullness of experience, the beauty of nature, and the voice of God can get lost in the chaos of our busy world and drifting thoughts.

Many of us also bear the burden of constantly allowing our minds to run off into the future. We speculate about what will happen or rest our hope on the achievement of some future state. I feel that I've missed a lot of my life focusing on what will happen in the future instead of living in and enjoying the here and now.

James wrote about this tendency.

> *Now listen, you who say, "Today or tomorrow we will go to this or that city, spend a year there, carry on business and make money." Why, you do not even know what will happen tomorrow. What is your life? You are a mist that appears for a little while and then vanishes (James 4:13-14).*

Many of us also think about and lament past experiences to further distract ourselves, but the Bible tells us to *"Forget the former things, do not dwell on the past"* (Isaiah 43:18).

You've probably heard about the concept of mindfulness. It's been all the rage recently. Mindfulness is noticing what you are doing, feeling, and thinking at the time you are actually doing, feeling, and thinking it. It involves operating fully in the present. Our bodies always operate in the present moment, but our minds don't have that limitation. I have previously confessed that mine wanders all over the place—through the past, to the future, and back to the present—all at lightning speed.

I frequently practice yoga. During the first six months or so that I practiced, my mind would be all over the place during final pose, when you are supposed to practice mindful meditation. I'd be thinking about all the things I needed to be doing and counting down the seconds until it was over. After ten plus years of yoga, I've gotten much better at the final pose (aka corpse pose). By the way, the corpse pose is my husband's favorite (and only) yoga pose.

Jesus encouraged us to be mindful and focus on the present: *"See how the flowers of the field grow. They do not labor or spin" (Matthew 6:28).* Through mindfulness, we can practice *"setting our minds on things above."* This allows us to practice paying attention to God and focusing on His kingdom.

Romans 12:2 instructs us as follows, *"Do not conform to the pattern of this world but be transformed by the renewing of your mind."* Through Christian mindfulness, we can spend time renewing our minds and not conforming to this world's multi-tasking, impatient, chaotic pattern.

Here are some practices which can help you to be more mindful:

Do physical activities that fully engage your mind

When you are engaged in physical activity, you can often clear your mind because your focus is on what you are doing. Bonus: It's also good for your body!

Set a reminder to focus on God

This could include setting an alarm or reminder on your cell phone, watch or calendar several times a day to remind you to take a moment to breathe or pray.

Meditate

This can be as simple as sitting and breathing for ten minutes and repeating a scripture. I sometimes just repeat the name Jesus to myself as I sit and breathe. This type of meditation helps us to be more centered and listen to God.

In the book, *The Purpose Driven Life*, Rick Warren describes meditation as follows:

"Meditation is focused thinking. It takes serious effort. You select a verse and reflect on it over and over in your mind...if you know how to worry, you already know how to meditate."

Further, he says: "No other habit can do more to transform your life and make you more like Jesus than daily reflection on Scripture...If you look up all the times God speaks about meditation in the Bible, you will be amazed at the benefits He has promised to those who take the time to reflect on His Word throughout the day."

You can also practice mindfulness in more informal ways throughout the day:

- Whenever you notice your mind wandering, bring it back to the present moment and take everything in through your senses.
- Pause periodically to breathe deeply.
- Take a walk and use it as a prompt to bring attention to the present, focusing on your surroundings and the sensations you feel.

Being more mindful can make a big difference in your life and relationships with God and other people.

REFLECT

- Are you currently practicing mindfulness?
- Try using some of the strategies listed to practice mindfulness for the next thirty days, and hopefully, it will then become a habit!

_____
_____
_____
_____
_____
_____
_____
_____
_____
_____
_____
_____
_____

38
Growth as a Mindset

My son, if you accept my words and store up my commands within you, turning your ear to wisdom and applying your heart to understanding—indeed, if you call out for insight and cry aloud for understanding, and if you look for it as for silver and search for it as for hidden treasures, then you will understand the fear of the Lord and find the knowledge of God (Proverbs 2:1-5).

Carol Dweck, a Stanford Professor of Psychology, has done a lot of research on mindset. She says that people adhere to one of two mindsets—a fixed mindset or a growth mindset. People with a fixed mindset operate under the belief that basic qualities like intelligence and talents are fixed traits. They hope that these traits will lead to success and don't seek to develop themselves further. As a result, they view their failures as a potential threat to their identity and have difficulty working through challenges. If a fixed mindset is left unchecked for too long, it can eventually lead people to believe that they simply can't overcome challenges.

People with a growth mindset operate under the belief that they can improve their intelligence and talents with passion, training, and deliberate effort. Someone with a growth mindset welcomes challenges and views failures or missteps as opportunities to learn and grow. For example, if you have a growth mindset, you may believe that you're gifted with a certain amount of intelligence, but that you can also constantly improve that level of intelligence. This will lead you to study, learn, and put the work into expanding your mind.

I'm certainly not a spring chicken. However, I most definitely want to adhere to a growth mindset in my life and continue learning and growing. Since I have embarked on the journey of studying God's word more diligently and writing, I have learned so much! I feel like each time I study and write about a topic, I gain more wisdom and come a little bit closer to being the person God wants me to be.

In Romans 12:2, Paul said that the renewing of our minds should transform us. If we have a fixed mindset, this renewing becomes impossible. If we adhere to a growth mindset, we believe that Christ can work in us and through us and transform us more into his likeness. A growth mindset also makes us more willing to take risks for God.

It's easy to get caught up in a fixed mindset in our relationship with God. We think that our faith is something static that we were born with, so we take God's grace for granted and don't work to strengthen our faith. Ultimately, believing that your relationship with God is set in stone is a rejection of His grace and a denial of His power. You need to actively participate in growing your faith and be open to His radical power to transform.

To move forward in a growth mindset, here are some things you can do:
- Pay attention to what you are telling yourself daily. Are the messages you are telling yourself growth-oriented or fixed?
- Reframe your thoughts. For example, instead of focusing on your mistake, reframe it and think of it as a learning opportunity.
- Look at challenges as opportunities to improve yourself.
- Don't view constructive feedback negatively. Use it positively to overcome limitations.
- Observe and learn from your mistakes as well as the mistakes of others.
- Attempt a variety of approaches rather than taking the same approach in each situation.
- Try not to be afraid to take calculated risks

Muhammed Ali said, "The man who views the world at 50 the same as he did at 20 has wasted 30 years of his life."

REFLECT

- Do you think you typically operate under a fixed mindset or growth mindset?
- How could you move further into a growth mindset to learn, grow, and build your relationship with our Savior?

_____
_____
_____
_____
_____
_____

39

Overthink Much?

Do you tend to overthink things? Consider what you should have said or done? Relive discussions or circumstances? Analyze mistakes in great detail? Get consumed with what-ifs or I should-haves? I used to do all of this all the time. But, like a fine wine, I have gotten better with age. There are some advantages to getting older. I finally realized that overthinking things was pointless and didn't add value in most situations.

It is important to have some insight into ourselves, our motives, our choices, our temptations, and our actions. So, a certain amount of self-evaluation can be good, but it can undoubtedly be overdone. Too much self-evaluation keeps us focused on ourselves and the things we should have done, ought to do, and will do. We dwell on our guilt, shame, and regrets when we overthink. Overthinking can also lead to depression, anxiety, an inability to move forward, and negatively impact our mental health.

The great thing about having a relationship with God is that we are never alone in our struggles, as evidenced by the Scriptures below:

- *"Come to me, all of you who are weary and burdened, and I will give you rest" (Matthew 11:28 CSB).*
- *"Cast all your anxiety on him because he cares for you" (1 Peter 5:7).*
- *"Do not be anxious about anything, but in every situation, by prayer and petition, with thanksgiving, present your requests to God" (Philippians 4:6).*

One of the things you can do to counteract overthinking is to take your thoughts captive and talk back to yourself. As I've said before, I'm not great at taking my thoughts captive, but I'm learning. I talk to myself a lot, and it helps! Learn the verses above by heart and tell them to yourself when you start to overthink.

Below are a few more thoughts and scriptures to add to your arsenal when you start to spiral into the overthinking trap:

- Jesus reminds us to pursue the Kingdom of God—the most important thing we can think about and pursue in our lives. This certainly puts our problems in perspective.

  But seek first his kingdom and his righteousness, and all these things will be given to you as well. Therefore do not worry about tomorrow, for tomorrow will worry about itself. Each day has enough trouble of its own (Matthew 6:33-34).

- Rather than dwell on all the things that have gone wrong, be grateful that God can use anything (even the situation you are overthinking) for your own good and His glory.

  "And we know that in all things God works for the good of those who love him, who have been called according to his purpose" (Romans 8:28).

As big as your particular problem or issue may seem, remember that it is only momentary in the grand scheme of things.

REFLECT

- Do you tend to overthink?
- Are there certain issues or situations that seem to suck you into the overthinking spiral?
- Which of the verses above will you add to your arsenal when you begin overthinking?

_____
_____
_____
_____
_____
_____
_____
_____
_____
_____
_____
_____
_____
_____
_____

40
What's Trust Got to Do with It?

"Trust in the Lord with all your heart, and do not lean on your own understanding. In all your ways acknowledge Him, and He will make straight your paths" (Proverbs 3:5-6 ESV).

I have found it helpful to select a word each year to focus my thoughts and actions. My word for this year is trust. I am focusing my energy this year on trusting God–an area where I definitely want and need to improve.

What exactly is trust? Trust is defined as a firm belief in the reliability, truth, ability, or strength of someone or something. Trusting God means that you believe that He loves you, will provide for you and that He is good.

I have spent too much of my life trusting in myself and other people. We are all human and inevitably will break trust from time to time. And I think it's been confirmed that I'm a hot mess, so trusting in myself is probably not the best idea. If I'm honest, there are times where I don't trust God as much as I should and turn to my own devices to try to fix or prevent problems. In fact, this happens quite a lot. Instead of trusting God, who has promised to be faithful to me, I trust in my own ability to guide and navigate circumstances. Of course, this rarely ends well. I usually end up feeling anxious and burdened and sometimes harm relationships in the process.

I wonder how drastically our lives would change if we completely trusted God with everything? I bet many mistakes and problems would be avoided, and our hopes and dreams would be realized more quickly and fully. Instead, we often grow impatient and opt for plan B, which will inevitably result in a letdown.

Here are some things that can help to increase our trust in God.

Make a habit of connecting with God

We can only grow in trust with a God we come to know. If you make connecting with God regularly a habit, this is the perfect way to learn how to trust Him more. Incorporate God into your daily routine by spending time with him, journaling, and attending church. Give him credit for the blessings in your life.

Trust in his wisdom and timing

> "Oh, the depth of the riches of the wisdom and knowledge of God! How unsearchable his judgments, and his paths beyond tracing out!" (Romans 11:33).

God knows best. Who are we to even think that we can take it upon ourselves to do a better job than Him in guiding our lives and circumstances? Or to trust other people to do the same? But we must remember that His timing is usually very different from ours. Many of us have spent a lot of time waiting on unanswered prayers. It's easy to lose trust when you've been waiting for healing, a spouse, a child, a better job, or financial security. But there is always a reason for God's delay. We must trust that His plan is still underway, even when we don't see evidence or feel like He is listening.

Pray!

Surrendering to God begins with our lips and our thoughts. We need more than a commitment to depend on Him; we need to cry out to Him to show dependence. When we pray, we admit that His ways are higher than ours. We show that we're leaving our troubles, burdens, and desires in His capable hands–instead of our grabby, faltering ones. Psalm 55:17 promises that when we reach out to Him, he hears us: *"Evening, morning, and noon I cry out in distress, and he hears my voice."*

Remind yourself of God's past faithfulness

Hebrews 13:8 says, *"Jesus Christ is the same yesterday and today and forever."*

This verse reminds us that God is absolutely unchanging. If He never changes and has been faithful to you in the past, then you can trust that he will be faithful in the future. Whenever you feel trust starting to fade, remind yourself of all the ways God has come through for you in the past. Even if He didn't come through in the way you thought He would, He likely came through in a bigger and better way.

Just today, I saw this in one of my favorite devotions, Jesus Calling by Sarah Young. Here is an excerpt:

> I want you to learn a new habit. Try saying, "I trust you Jesus" in response to whatever happens to you. This simple practice will help you see Me in every situation, acknowledging my sovereign control over the universe. When you view events from this perspective—through the light of my eternal presence—fear loses its grip on you.

The Scriptures below will help to confirm that we can trust God! I am going to keep them close as I focus on building trust this year.

- *"May you be richly rewarded by the Lord, the God of Israel, under whose wings you have come to take refuge" (Ruth 2:12).*
- *"My God is my rock, in whom I take refuge" (2 Samuel 22:3 BSB).*
- *"…He answered their prayers, because they trusted in him" (1 Chronicles 5:20).*
- *"But blessed is the one who trusts in the Lord, whose confidence is in him" (Jeremiah 17:7).*
- *"Those who know your name trust in you, for you, Lord, have never forsaken those who seek you" (Psalm 9:10).*

REFLECT

- How are you doing with trusting God in your life?
- What will you do to trust Him more?

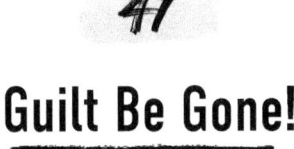

Guilt Be Gone!

"For God did not send His Son into the world to condemn the world, but to save the world through him" (John 3:17).

Do you spend much of your time feeling guilty? I know I do. We have salvation and forgiveness through Jesus, but many of us still tend to feel guilty. So, what exactly is guilt? It is the failure to do what you ought to have done—or sometimes it can be the failure to do what you THINK you ought to have done.

I remember feeling a lot of guilt when my children were growing up. I was working, and I wasn't spending as much time with them as I thought I should. This type of guilt is a little ridiculous. It zaps your energy and poisons your mind when there is probably little that you can do to change it. I was basically a single mom and had to work to help provide for my children. On the flip side, I felt guilty because I didn't think I was working enough!

Many of us live with a pervasive, low-level sense of guilt because we feel bad about all of the things we aren't doing or the things we aren't doing as well as we'd like. I feel like I have LGGD (low-grade guilt disorder) much of the time. This is not an actual medical term, by the way. Here are some of the reasons we may feel this type of guilt:

* I should pray more.
* I watch movies and television too often.
* I don't spend enough time with God.
* I don't give enough.
* I should volunteer or help others more.
* I went shopping and bought stuff that I shouldn't have (this is a biggie for me!).
* I should eat more healthy foods.
* I don't exercise enough.

- I could use my time better.
- I should work more.
- I should work less.
- I don't pay enough attention to my kids or spouse.

Cumulatively, these things can make us feel like we are generally a disappointment. And, more often than not, this type of guilt isn't based on things that are necessarily wrong but on our own personal expectations. Just today, I skipped church. Why? Because I was having hot flashes last night and didn't sleep well. The old me would be so hard on myself that I would be envisioning hot flashes in a place that is permanently hot. If you have LGGD, try not to be so hard on yourself and ask God for His help.

Another type of guilt occurs when we sin. When we sin (and notice I say "when" and not "if"), we should feel sorry for what we did and ask for forgiveness. Jesus has taken on our guilt on the cross. When we repent for our sins, God forgives us, and our guilt should be gone.

Romans 8:1 says there is *"no condemnation for those who are in Christ Jesus."*

At times, we may be inclined to hang on to our sins after the Lord has forgiven us. Satan often uses guilt to keep us from God. After we receive forgiveness and are moving forward, Satan will try to pull us back and say, "Where do you think you're going? Remember what you did?" Then, those feelings of guilt and shame come flooding back. When this happens, remind yourself that this guilt isn't from God and tell Satan to take a hike!

Here are some practical steps that you can take to overcome guilt:

- If it's LGGD, get over it. It's not productive and healthy.
- If your guilt is based on a specific sin or incident, confess your sin and repent. *"If we confess our sins, he is faithful and just and will forgive us our sins and purify us from all unrighteousness"* (1 John 1:9)
- Thank God for His grace and forgiveness.
- If your guilt returns, remind yourself that your sins are forgiven!

But because of his great love for us, God, who is rich in mercy, made us alive with Christ even though we were dead in transgressions—it is by grace you have been saved. And God raised us up with Christ and seated us in the heavenly realms in Christ Jesus, in order that in the coming ages he might show the incomparable riches of his grace, expressed in his kindness to us in Christ Jesus. For it is by grace you have been saved, through faith—and this is not from yourselves, it is a gift of God (Ephesians 2:4-8).

REFLECT

- What do you feel guilty about?
- Have you asked for forgiveness and repented (if guilt is based on sin)? If not, do it!
- What can you do to let your guilt go, knowing that Jesus took care of it on the cross?

42

Jesus Take the Wheel

I love the song "Jesus Take the Wheel" by Carrie Underwood. It shares some great wisdom to live by! I want Jesus to take the wheel in my life but often struggle with surrendering to Him. So, what exactly does it mean to surrender? Surrender means to yield ownership, to relinquish control over what we consider to be ours. This could include everything from our possessions, to our time, to our family. When we surrender to God, we acknowledge that what we think is ours belongs to Him and that He is in control of everything. Surrendering to God helps us let go of whatever has held us back from His best for our lives. It's not always easy, but it is a choice that we must make daily.

In *The Purpose Driven Life*, Rick Warren says that everyone surrenders to something—if not God, then other people, money, fear, pride, or lust. He says that if you don't surrender to Christ, you surrender to chaos.

Jesus tells us to deny ourselves. This means that we are to surrender our will and follow His no matter what the cost. Matthew 16:24 (ESV) says, *"If anyone would come after me, let him deny himself and take up his cross and follow me."* In Matthew 4:19 (BSB), Jesus tells Peter and Andrew, *"Come, follow me…and I will make you fishers of men."* They immediately left their nets and followed him.

Can you honestly say that you have fully surrendered all areas of your life to Him? I know I haven't, but I sure do want to! As I've said before, I struggle with surrendering my children to Him. I think about what strong faith Abraham had in surrendering his son, Isaac. As a result of his faith, he ultimately didn't have to.

What if we don't surrender? Matthew 16:25 (ESV) provides a warning for us: *"For whoever would save his life will lose it, but whoever loses his life for my sake will find it."* To me, this means that anyone who pursues his/her own interests and rejects Jesus will live a shallow, meaningless life and eternity apart from him.

Surrender is one of the most difficult challenges of our lives as Christians. It involves giving up all of our hopes, dreams, and fears to God. But we won't ever have peace if we don't fully surrender to God. Job 22:21 says, *"Submit to God and be at peace with him; in this way prosperity will come to you."*

In Galatians 2:20, Paul provides a great example of what it means to surrender to God: *"I have been crucified with Christ and I no longer live, but Christ lives in me. The life I now live in the body, I live by faith in the Son of God, who loved me and gave himself for me."*

REFLECT

- Are there areas in your life where you have not surrendered to God? If so, what are they?
- What actions can you take to surrender these areas to Him?

Section 4:

Hot Mess Issues

Leslie Speas

43
I Am a Recovering People-Pleaser

"Am I now trying to win the approval of human beings, or of God? Or am I trying to please people? If I were still trying to please people, I would not be a servant of Christ" (Galatians 1:10).

My name is Leslie, and I'm a recovering "people-pleaser." For most of my life, I have been overly concerned about whether people liked me and looked for affirmation of my worth from others. There is an old adage that I believe to be true that says you will never please all of the people all the time—and if you try, you will inevitably suffer in the process.

People-pleasers try to prove that they are valuable by pleasing others—and, in attempting to do so, quiet the voice within that says they aren't valuable. They believe that the approval of others will fill them, confirm them, and satisfy them. People-pleasing often requires saying yes to things we probably shouldn't and trying to perform perfectly to not disappoint others. People-pleasers feel that a failure to please will result in rejection, and they will no longer be valuable.

If your answer is yes to most of these questions, you likely suffer from people-pleasing:

- Do you accept responsibility for the happiness of others?
- Do you believe you can make others happy?
- Do you feel guilty when you think of yourself instead of others?
- Do you feel guilty when you tell someone no?
- Do you feel guilty when you think of yourself, your health, and your emotional well-being?
- Do you feel better about yourself when you give in to the desires of others rather than pleasing yourself?

I used to be an extreme people-pleaser. Thankfully, I am less concerned about whether others like me than I used to be. However, it still makes me feel good when I think that I have gained others' approval. In my younger days, I wasn't good at setting boundaries to ensure that I cared for my soul. I have gotten much better at filtering requests through what is most important in my life. However, it still upsets me quite a bit when I feel I have disappointed someone else or think they don't like me. I mean, what's not to like? So clearly, I'm not totally over my people-pleasing tendencies. *"Woe to you when everyone speaks well of you, for that is how their ancestors treated the false prophets" (Luke 6:26)*. I like the Message version's translation of this:

> *There's trouble ahead when you live only for the approval of others, saying what flatters them, doing what indulges them. Popularity contests are not truth contests—look how many scoundrel preachers were approved by your ancestors! Your task is to be true, not popular.*

In *The Best Yes*, LysaTerKeurst says there are three D's that can tell you if you are in people-pleasing mode:

- **Dread –** you say yes to something or someone but internally feel a sense of dread.
- **Disappointment –** Every yes requires that you say no to something else, which then can result in disappointment for you or others.
- **Drama –** The dread and disappointment are likely going to create drama in your life.

She suggests pausing before you make an impulsive decision to think through the three D's, and ask yourself if you are doing whatever it is to impress someone or prove something.

If you are a people-pleaser, you should try to redirect your need to please others to focus more on what pleases God. Try to stop worrying so much about what others think or feel about you and do what you feel God wants you to do. I know this is easier said than done but look for prompting from the Holy Spirit on what you should and shouldn't do.

Setting boundaries and designating time in your schedule to nurture your relationship with God can help you overcome the people-pleasing cycle. Remember that you are valuable for who you are in Christ, not in other people's opinions of you.

> *"Be careful not to practice your righteousness in front of others to be seen by them. If you do, you will have no reward from your Father in heaven" (Matthew 6:1).*

REFLECT

- Are you a people-pleaser?
- How can you use the three D's to help guide your actions?
- What actions will you take to focus more on pleasing God than pleasing other people?

44
Perfectly Imperfect

"It is God who arms me with strength and makes my way clear" (Psalm 18:32 BSB).

Are you a perfectionist? Think about these questions. Do you:
- Often worry that you said or did the wrong thing?
- Read too much into others' comments?
- Worry that you dropped the ball?
- Worry about looking good to other people?
- Overthink things?
- Beat yourself up when you make a mistake or receive correction?

A perfectionist regards anything short of perfection as unacceptable. This may involve setting unrealistically demanding goals accompanied by the tendency to regard failure to achieve them as unacceptable and a sign of personal worthlessness.

It's not bad to strive to be perfect, is it? It seems that it might motivate us to try to be our best. This is absolutely not accurate. We are human and will never achieve perfection, so the quest for it is exhausting. If we let it, perfectionism will gradually erode our inner peace and rob us of our joy.

Perfectionism comes from a place of fear that we may be seen with all of our faults and failures. In *The Gifts of Imperfection: Let Go of Who You Think You're Supposed to Be and Embrace Who You Are*, Dr. Brené Brown brings to light an important point, stating that "perfectionism is not about healthy striving, it is a thought process that says if I do these things perfectly, I can avoid shame, blame, and judgment."

Below are a few suggested strategies that might help in overcoming perfectionism:

See mistakes and failures in a positive light

One of the things that has been most impactful for me in my quest to overcome perfectionism is the understanding and acknowledgment that we all make mistakes and that it's okay. We all fail from time to time, and it doesn't mean that we are not worthy. Instead, it allows us to learn, grow, and ask God for help.

Meditate on God's love for you

Look for and record Bible verses to remind you of God's love for you and all of the ways He proves that love.

Set realistic expectations

Be kind to yourself and set realistic goals that you can achieve, celebrating your successes along the way. Instead of beating yourself up because you didn't lose ten pounds in a month (probably an unrealistic goal), set more realistic expectations for yourself, and celebrate along the way as you achieve them. In this example, you might set a goal of losing a pound a week.

Alter your self-talk

When you hear that critical voice in your head telling you that your work isn't good enough or you aren't good enough, shut it down. As I've mentioned before, I sometimes say, "Get away, Satan," to myself to redirect my brain. Being aware of your perfectionistic tendencies can help you to redirect yourself in a positive direction.

Remember that Jesus never demanded perfection from us. He simply asked us to lay down all of our baggage, pick up our cross, and follow Him.

REFLECT

- Do you tend to be a perfectionist?
- If so, what will you do to overcome this tendency?

_____
_____
_____
_____
_____
_____
_____
_____

45

Managing My Image

"Fear of man will prove to be a snare, but whoever trusts in the Lord is kept safe" (Proverbs 29:25).

In the book *Free of Me: Why Life is Better When It's Not About You*, Sharon Hodde Miller talks about the concept of image management. She says that this is when you "manage" how people see you and treat everything in your life as if it were a reflection of you. I've got to quit reading so much as it keeps adding to my list of things I need to work on.

Sharon Hodde Miller says that when our spouse or kids become extensions of us, they are forced to bear a burden that was never theirs to carry. I don't think this is much of an issue with my husband, except when he wears his stupid rain hat. Oh, and his mowing outfit. These things don't do much for my image or his. However, I know for sure that I have treated my kids as extensions of myself at times, seeing myself, my aspirations, and my fears rather than who they are and what they need. Boy, did I try hard to get one of them to be a Physical Therapist, something that I wish I had done. And I tried to keep them from failing, which is one of the worst mistakes I made as a parent. They have to fail to learn and grow into responsible adults.

When my kids were younger, I often felt like what they did (or didn't do) related to my parenting or was a reflection on me. My youngest daughter didn't potty train until she was almost four; my oldest didn't walk until about sixteen months. Now it's nothing, but at the time, it stressed me out, and I wondered what I wasn't doing that I should be. We want to be good parents and put pressure on our kids to be successful. Kids are starting dance and sports earlier and earlier, often for the parents rather than for them. After all, they need to start early to be a professional athlete or ballerina, right?

Now that my children are in their twenties, I am still having a tough time letting go of what I thought they should/would be and do, reconciling myself to the paths they are taking. I know for sure that I need to let go and that I can't control their directions in their lives, but I sure want to try. And I wonder how much of this is really about me.

When managing our image is involved in our parenting, our kids become responsible for their reputation, insecurities, and fears as well as ours. This would also apply to a spouse, friend, or family member who we involve in our image management. Joshua 24:15 says, "...*But as for me and my household, we will serve the Lord.*" This indicates that our purpose is to love God and love others. It isn't for us to look good or raise successful kids in the eyes of the world.

I found this poem online that relates to this topic, and I thought I'd share:

> Your children are not your children.
> They are the sons and daughters of Life's longing for itself.
> They come through you but not from you,
> And though they are with you yet they belong not to you.
> You may give them your love but not your thoughts,
> For they have their own thoughts.
> You may house their bodies but not their souls,
> For their souls dwell in the house of tomorrow,
> which you cannot visit, not even in your dreams.
> You may strive to be like them,
> but seek not to make them like you.
> For life goes not backward nor tarries with yesterday.
>
> Words from a poem by Kahlil Gibran

REFLECT

- Is image management an issue for you? If so, in what way?

- What actions could you take to overcome this tendency to manage your image?

_____
_____
_____
_____
_____
_____
_____
_____
_____
_____
_____
_____
_____

46
The Secret to Parenting

"Direct your children onto the right path, and when they are older, they will not leave it" (Proverbs 22:6 NLT).

Have you ever wanted to know the secret to parenting? I sure wish I did. I'd slap a patent on it for sure. We are always looking for a silver bullet, aren't we? Most times, there isn't one. So, what about parenting? What do we need to do to be good parents?

First of all, let me say that I am definitely no expert in this area. Parenting is the hardest thing I've ever done. I have diligently tried, but I'm not sure that I have done it that well. But I did raise two daughters and was involved in raising two stepdaughters. Surprisingly, they all have survived so far. Let me just say that it was not easy with four girls, particularly during middle school.

I will probably get off the path a few times in this chapter but let me just say that step-parenting is quite difficult. You don't feel like you have the authority to do much in terms of discipline, and it's often difficult to navigate, especially when the kids aren't receptive. I remember finding a notebook under my stepdaughter's bed that said, "ways to break up Leslie and Dad," with a list of ideas, some that had been implemented. And this isn't that relevant but funny: We found my other stepdaughter's diary, which said, "may whoever reads this have explosive poop," on the first page. Cracked me up.

When children are little, they are sweet, cuddly, and dependent on you for just about everything. Then, they begin to grow and go through stages such as walking, talking, potty training (which I was terrible at for kids–and puppies), starting school, getting their driver's license, etc. Our parenting evolves until they finally leave the nest and are ultimately left to navigate their own path. You wonder: Did I do enough? Did I teach them enough to survive on their own? Did I give them enough foundation in faith to weather the storms of life? And my personal go-to: How bad did I screw them up?

My kids are in their twenties, and I thought I'd be on cruise control, but that hasn't been the case. Parenting adult kids is harder than at any other point–in my experience, anyway. I guess parenting never really ends. I believe that I hurt more than they do when they are suffering or going through a difficult challenge.

I don't know the secret to parenting, but here are some tips from research and a few from experience:

Give them unconditional love

God loves us unconditionally. Thank goodness it's a love that isn't based on our behavior but on His nature. We certainly don't deserve it, but He never withholds it from us. In the same way, I think that we should also show our children unconditional love. First John 3:12 says, *"See what great love the Father has lavished on us, that we should be called children of God! And that is what we are! The reason the world does not know us is that it did not know him."*

Realize that there isn't one way to parent

All children are different and require a "customized" version of parenting. Know your child's love language. If you don't, there is a book for that! We were each created to be unique, and we are motivated by different things. Recognize your child's special gifts and passions—and provide opportunities for your child to grow in these areas.

Provide your children with a good Christian foundation

Help to lay the foundation for your children by educating them about the Bible and praying with and for them. Ideally, you are involved in a church or Christian group where your children can establish roots and grow in their faith. Three of our kids didn't engage much in the youth group at church. I wish that I had pushed the issue more. It was a very meaningful experience for the one that did.

Empower your children and allow them to fail

Life is full of trials and hardships. I spent a lot of time and effort trying to protect my children from going through difficulties. Of course, they went through some by default, but I involved myself when I shouldn't have at times to try to protect them (#helicoptermom). My oldest daughter went off to college not knowing how to do laundry, cook (of course, no one wanted me to teach her that), and a whole host of other things. She was perfectly fine to have me handle whatever I was willing to do for her, whereas my younger daughter was very independent and took it upon herself to get things done. I should have pressed and encouraged my oldest daughter to be more independent and do more for herself.

Be a good role model

I know that, as a parent, I have sometimes operated under "do as I say, not as I do." Know that your children are constantly watching your actions and reactions and learning from you. Demonstrate integrity, kindness, generosity, patience, and compassion. Show them that you are trying to live your life as Jesus would want you to. Be a role model for hard work and instill in them a positive work ethic. These verses show us the importance of being a good role model:

- *"…but set an example for the believers in speech, in conduct, in love, in faith and in purity" (1 Timothy 4:12).*
- *"Show yourself in all respects to be a model of good works, and in your teaching show integrity, dignity" (Titus 2:7 ESV).*

<u>Prayerfully discipline your children</u>

I believe that children want and need boundaries. Hold your children accountable for their actions and behavior, but not in a demeaning or hurtful way. At times, I would ignore my children's bad behavior or failure to listen. Remember counting to ten? I'd often count to ten several times before doing anything. The result would generally involve yelling. Sometimes I would also ignore things they did because I was tired or just didn't feel like dealing with it.

When they were little, it was hard to discipline them because they were so stinkin' cute. My younger daughter had imaginary friends—a lion was one of them. She would often throw a fit when we would get in the car to go somewhere because she said we forgot the lion. I'd go back into the house and come back out, pretending that I had him with me. She would smile knowingly, probably thinking, "Sucker!" And there was another invisible friend she called Clyde, the snake. Precursor for things to come since she now has a snake.

Anyhow, you should discipline your kids when appropriate, even if they are cute. Start 'em young! Consider these verses:

- *"Discipline your children while there is hope. Otherwise you will ruin their lives" (Proverbs 19:18 NLT).*
- *"Fathers, do not provoke your children to anger by the way you treat them. Rather, bring them up with the discipline and instruction that comes from the Lord" (Ephesians 6:4 NLT).*

<u>Parent in partnership with God</u>

Invite God to guide you in parenting your children. I went through periods in the "wilderness" of my faith as my children were growing up. As a result, I tried to parent using my own devices most of the time. My children's father wasn't a very consistent presence in their lives, so I tried to do it all. If I had prayed and let God lead the way, I would have made better decisions and would have been more successful at parenting. I am undoubtedly doing a better job of partnering with Him now, so it's never too late! *"Trust in the Lord with all your heart; do not depend on your own understanding. Seek his will in all you do, and he will show you which path to take" (Proverbs 3:5-6 NLT).*

In conclusion, realize that God gives us the privilege of raising our children for a short while—but they ultimately belong to Him. They are meant to be loved, nurtured, and returned unto Him.

REFLECT

- Which of these things do you need to work on as it relates to your parenting?
- What will you do to make this happen?

47

It's Hard to Be Humble

…"God opposes the proud but shows favor to the humble." Submit yourselves, then, to God. Resist the devil, and he will flee from you. Come near to God and He will come near to you. Wash your hands, you sinners, and purify your hearts, you double-minded…Humble yourselves before the Lord, and he will lift you up (James 4:6-8,10).

Do you remember this song? "Oh Lord, it's hard to be humble when you're perfect in every way. I can't wait to look in the mirror, I get better lookin' each day".

Probably many of you don't, as I think it was from 1980. I wish I could remember other important things as well as I remember song lyrics from the eighties. But back to our topic, it's indeed hard to be humble. I always thought I was a humble person until I did more research on the sin of pride.

Here are a few examples of pride in action. A prideful person:
1. Insists on arguing his/her point and won't listen to anyone else
2. Has trouble with correction, is defensive, always has an excuse, or blames others
3. Finds fault with others
4. Craves superiority over others
5. Thinks he/she can carry his/her own burdens
6. Judges others
7. Is desperate for attention and/or has a strong desire to be admired
8. Thinks that he/she can handle things better than God

Uh oh. I see myself in a few of those, especially five and eight.

Today, pride is often celebrated as a virtue. We have pride in our work, our children, and our culture, among many other things. Pride is defined as an excessive belief in one's own abilities that interferes with his/her recognition of the grace of God. Pride is also known as vanity. C.S. Lewis called pride the great sin and the devil's most effective and destructive tool.

Humility is knowing the truth about yourself and your proper standing with God. It's accepting that you are weak and that your heart is beyond your understanding. It is acknowledging that you have a creator who knows you better than you know yourself. It is freedom from pride or arrogance.

Humility is often seen as a weakness, but this is a misconception. It is associated with quietness, submission, and thoughts of inadequacy, but it does not mean that you should bow down or be subservient to other people. God wants us to possess humility. A humble person has a gentle spirit and thinks soberly about his/herself. This means that we don't brag about our accomplishments and abilities. Rather, we acknowledge that our sufficiency is of God in all things. (2 Corinthians 3:5) Proverbs 11:2 says, *"When pride comes, then comes disgrace, but with humility comes wisdom."*

I like C.S. Lewis' definition of humility, "Humility is not thinking less of ourselves, but thinking of ourselves less." Here are some behaviors that you will see in humble people. A humble person:

- Puts others first.
- Listens and seeks to understand.
- Says thank you and shows gratitude.
- Seeks input and feedback from others.
- Takes responsibility and admits mistakes.
- Shows curiosity
- Is willing to ask for help
- Realizes that all things come from God

If we are honest, almost all of us suffer from pride at one time or another. If you sense pride in your life, ask the Lord to help you put others before yourself.

REFLECT

- Are you guilty of the sin of pride? In what way? Don't feel bad; most of us are!
- What actions can you take to show more humility in your life?

48
Pompously Prideful

As I said in the last lesson, I have never thought of myself as prideful. But after learning more about pride, I'm sorry to say that this isn't always the case. Let's explore pride a little deeper. Pride is defined as a high or inordinate opinion of one's own dignity, importance, merit, or superiority, whether as cherished in the mind or as displayed in conduct. Further, pride is a state of mind or, more essentially, a condition of the heart in which a person has replaced the rule of God over his life with the rule of his own will. This is where I struggle the most. I often get in there and try to intervene in His plans, acting as if I'm in control.

Pride has been called the "original sin" that is the root of every other sin. C.S. Lewis said that pride "is the complete anti-God state of mind."

Pride is the root of many other sins such as:

- **Jealousy-** the resentful awareness of an advantage enjoyed by another that we feel should rightfully be ours.

- **Bitterness-** that unpleasant, lingering feeling when someone has offended us, deceived us, or failed to deliver on what we thought they owed us.

- **Strife-** the competitive craving to be number one, including the desire for power, authority, and praise.

- **Deceitfulness-** lying or misleading others by hiding something that we think may make us look bad.

- **Hypocrisy-** pretending to be something we are not because we fear being seen and known for who we really are.

- **Slander-** speaking negatively of others to make ourselves look or feel better.

- **Greed-** desiring more for ourselves than God wishes or permits.

It was the sin of pride which transformed Lucifer, the anointed cherub of God, into Satan. The sin of pride also led Eve to eat the forbidden fruit. (Genesis 3)

There are many other examples of pride in the Bible. Here are a few:
- King David struggled with pride when he called for an unnecessary census of Israel's warriors. He trusted more in a strong army rather than in an all-powerful God. God was displeased with the census and punished Israel because of it (1 Chronicles 21).

- King Uzziah presumed himself worthy of priestly duties. He was unfaithful and entered the temple of the Lord to burn incense on the altar. As a result, he was cursed with leprosy (2 Chronicles 26:16).

- King Hezekiah became very ill. He prayed, and the Lord answered him, giving him a miraculous sign. His heart was proud, and he did not respond to God's answer, so the Lord's wrath was upon him (2 Chronicles 32:24-25).

- King Nebuchadnezzar let his pride get in the way and took credit for building Babylon. As a result, he was driven from his kingdom (1 Chronicles 29:11).

- Herod assumed the status of a god rather than praising the One True God. As a result, he was struck dead and eaten by worms (Acts 12:20-23).

Some rather unpleasant outcomes—especially the worm one! What's the lesson here? God is quite able to humble the proud and won't hesitate to do so. What else does the Bible say about pride? Here are a few examples:
- *"To fear the Lord is to hate evil; I hate pride and arrogance, evil behavior and perverse speech" (Proverbs 8:13).*

- *"Do not keep talking so proudly or let your mouth speak such arrogance, for the Lord is a God who knows, and by him deeds are weighed" (1 Samuel 2:3).*

- *"Pride goes before destruction, a haughty spirit before a fall" (Proverbs 16:18).*

- *"Pride only breeds quarrels, but wisdom is found in those who take advice" (Proverbs 13:10).*

James 4:6 (ESV) says, *"God opposes the proud but gives grace to the humble."* This doesn't say that God simply ignores the proud. He works in open opposition against them! Pride provokes God to wrath and indignation; it irritates him, agitates him, and displeases him. So, are you convinced yet that pride is an issue that we should avoid at all costs?

Here are some things that we can do to help us to overcome pride and live with humility.

- **Pray.** Ask God to reveal and remove pride in our hearts, minds, and lives.
- **Read the Bible and do what it says.** For us to hear God, we have to listen to His Word and be obedient to it.
- **Repent.** To keep pride at bay in our lives, we must continually confess and repent of our sins.
- **Serve others.** If we serve others, we can stay humble and avoid pride.
- **Take your prideful thoughts captive.** Do what we are instructed to do in Philippians 4:8:

    Finally brothers and sisters, whatever is true, whatever is noble, whatever is right, whatever is pure, whatever is lovely, whatever is admirable—if anything is excellent or praiseworthy—think about such things.

REFLECT

- How does pride manifest itself in your life?
- What will you do to overcome the tendency to be prideful?

_____
_____
_____
_____
_____
_____
_____
_____
_____
_____
_____
_____
_____
_____

49

American Idol

"Son of man, these men have set up idols in their hearts and put wicked stumbling blocks before their faces" (Ezekiel 14:3).

Back in the day, idols were often little statues that people worshipped. Today, idols are now typically things that we can't see. An idol is anything that we run to for comfort when our souls really need God. An idol can be anything that claims our affections, time, money, thoughts, or desires and takes precedence over God. There are many examples—youthfulness, children, fame, money, relationships, social media, sex, drugs, approval, and gluttony, to name a few. We even idolize musicians and celebrities, as in the American Idol example. Colossians 3:5 tells us not to be greedy for the good things of this life, for that is idolatry.

Idolatry is certainly not new. It began with Adam and Eve when they ate the fruit. They certainly didn't lack anything. They did it because an idol formed in their hearts, and they wanted to be like God.

I have a very strange idol—exercise. What a weirdo I am. Most people don't even like to exercise, and I don't always want to either. However, I feel that I must exercise every day and start feeling anxious if I don't. This infatuation with exercise and my weight began in college and has persisted throughout my adult life. I sometimes let my preoccupation with fitness infringe upon the time that I could be spending with God.

> *…Therefore watch yourselves very carefully, so that you do not become corrupt and make for yourselves an idol, an image of any shape…. And when you look up to the sky and see the sun, the moon, and stars—all the heavenly array—do not be enticed into bowing down to them and worshipping the things the Lord your God has apportioned to all of the nations under heaven (Deuteronomy 4:15-16, 19).*

God is jealous when we turn to idols. He wants us to be all in with Him rather than spending our lives seeking the world's empty pleasures. He wants our time and attention, as indicated in the Scriptures below.

- *"For the Lord your God is a consuming fire, a jealous God"* (Deuteronomy 4:24).

CONFESSIONS OF A HOT MESS- FROM MESS TO MESSAGE

* *"They made him jealous with their foreign gods and angered him with their detestable idols"* (Deuteronomy 32:16).

What are your idols? You may know right off, or it may require a little thought. You can get an idea by answering some of the following questions:

I need _____.

I fear _____.

I am preoccupied by _____.

I take refuge in _____.

Once you have taken the time to identify your idols, you can work to overcome them. Idols don't love us, but Jesus does. Confess and ask Jesus to replace any idols with himself.

REFLECT

* What are your idols?
* What can you do to overcome your idols and focus on God?

_____
_____
_____
_____
_____
_____
_____
_____
_____
_____
_____
_____
_____
_____
_____
_____
_____
_____

50

I Deserve More!

"People will be lovers of themselves, lovers of money, boastful, proud, abusive, disobedient to their parents, ungrateful, unholy" (2 Timothy 3:2).

Have you ever felt like you are entitled to more? A bigger house? A better car? A higher-paying job? I know that I have felt this way at times. The other day, I saw an image that showed a blank sheet of paper and said, "a comprehensive list of what the world owes you." This is so true! The world owes us nothing. Christ is the only one who has ever been truly entitled. And, as sinners, the only thing that we deserve is God's judgment.

Entitlement is the belief that we inherently deserve privileges or special treatment or that we have the right to something. Two attitudes make up entitlement:
1. I am exempt from responsibility
2. I am owed special treatment.

This kind of self-focus leads to selfish and narcissistic behavior.

Here are a few examples of an attitude of entitlement:
- I deserve to have children, so why am I struggling?
- I deserve to have a spouse, so why don't I?
- I work hard, so why am I not getting promoted?

Many of us have been frustrated by people who feel they deserve to have things handed over to them with very little effort. Through my work in Human Resources, I see this often with people who have easy availability to jobs but try to "work the system." The stories I could tell! In general, I think we also see this attitude with the millennial generation more than with previous generations. Perhaps, this is because we as parents have led them to believe that they were entitled to certain things. They often were awarded trophies, even when they didn't win.

Matthew 20 tells the story of a landowner. He went out early in the morning and hired workers and agreed to pay them a denarius. He hired other workers later in the day, even as late as five in the afternoon. That evening, he paid everyone a denarius regardless of what time they began work. Needless to say, the workers who started earlier were a little disgruntled. The landowner said,

> ... Friend, I am not being unfair to you. Didn't you agree to work for a denarius? Take your pay and go. I want to give the one who was hired last the same as I gave you. Don't I have the right to do what I want with my own money? Or are you envious because I am generous? So the last will be first, and the first will be last (Matthew 20:13-16).

In this story, the landowner is the only one worthy to decide what's fair. This story illustrates that God can be trusted even when it seems unfair to us.

What can we do when we are feeling entitled?

- **Own the behavior.** Recognize the presence of entitlement and analyze why you feel that way. Remind yourself that you aren't entitled to anything.

- **Get your eyes off yourself and focus on helping others.** Nothing can change your attitude quicker than helping someone else. It often can also give you perspective on how good you have it.

- **Understand that life is not fair.** Life can be beautiful. Unfortunately, it's not always fair (at least by our worldly standards). We don't get to choose our parents or lots of other things in this life. Bad things happen to good people. Find ways to make the most out of what God has given you.

REFLECT

- Are you guilty of feeling entitled at times? Think about what makes you feel that way.

- What will you do to overcome feelings of entitlement?

51

Praying Out Loud Challenged

"Let us then approach the throne of grace with confidence, so that we may receive mercy and find grace to help us in our time of need" (Hebrews 4:16 BSB).

Does anyone else struggle with prayer? I sure do. My biggest struggle is praying out loud with a group. I don't think I'm the only one because there is always that question, "Would anyone like to close us in prayer?" Usually, crickets. Some people pray so eloquently that you'd think they must have a Ph.D. in prayer and make you feel even less adequate.

Not only do I struggle with praying out loud, but I also struggle with individual prayer. I've mentioned my crazy mind before. It's all over the place when I pray and often goes down a rabbit hole, and I lose focus. Other times I try to correct myself because I feel that my prayers are out of order. I'm not sure why we tend to get so legalistic about prayer. Finally, sometimes I take a "prayer nap" where I fall asleep amid my prayers.

In *The Power of a Simple Prayer,* Joyce Meyer says:

> Prayer is the way we partner with God to see His plans and purposes come to pass in our lives and in the lives of those we love. It is the means by which human beings on earth can actually enter into the awesome presence of God. It allows us to share our hearts with Him, to listen for His voice, and to know how to discover and enjoy all the great things He has for us.

I have read that it can be helpful and effective to approach Jesus as a friend– to stop praying and start talking. Engage Him throughout the day with short messages, inviting Him to share your life as you go throughout your daily activities. Just like our close relationships are maintained by spending time together, so is our relationship with Jesus.

I think many people feel that they need to be in a "prayer position" to pray. I have learned that it can be just as effective to pray when driving or walking in nature. I don't believe it's necessary to be on your knees with hands in a prayer position to have a fulfilling prayer life.

I believe that we tend to overcomplicate prayer—and Satan helps us with that, I'm sure. Prayers can be simple and can be distilled down as follows:

- **Wow** - praising Him
- **Thanks** - showing gratitude
- **Forgive** - forgive me for my sins
- **Help** - help with my needs
- **Please** - please help my friend/family member

"The fewer the words, the better the prayer," said Martin Luther. This reassures us that we can talk to God in everyday language, just like talking to a friend. My favorite is "Help!"

If you struggle with prayer, one thing that has helped me is to start reading my Bible and ask myself questions like:

- Is there something here I should be thankful for?
- Is there something here that names a sin I should ask forgiveness for?
- Am I struggling with something in this passage and need to ask for strength?
- Is someone I know struggling with something in this passage?

It's also been helpful for me to make notes about what I will address in prayer in a prayer journal. Another thing that has helped slow down my crazy mind is taking deep breaths before praying to get centered. This helps me to stay more focused.

When you don't know what to pray, the Holy Spirit will help. Romans 8:26 provides some wonderful encouragement about prayer. *"In the same way, the Spirit helps us in our weakness. We do not know what we ought to pray for, but the Spirit himself intercedes for us through wordless groans."*

Luke 11:9 teaches us more about prayer:
So I say to you: Ask and it will be given to you; seek and you will find; knock and the door will be opened to you. For everyone who asks receives; the one who seeks finds; and the one who knocks, the door will be opened.

Prayer is our opportunity to spend time with God and develop a deeper relationship with him. It also opens the door for God to work in our lives. Let's keep it simple and try not to overcomplicate it. I think the result will be a richer prayer life and an enhanced understanding of the heart of God.

REFLECT

- Do you sometimes struggle with prayer?
- What has helped you when you have been at your best in your prayer life?
- What will you do to improve your prayer life going forward?

52

When You Doubt...

Do you not know? Have you not heard? The Lord is the everlasting God, the Creator of the ends of the earth. He will not grow tired or weary, and his understanding no one can fathom. He gives strength to the weary and increases the power of the weak (Isaiah 40:28-29).

Do you struggle with doubt? If we are honest, probably most of us have at one time or another. We may doubt for intellectual reasons. Or maybe we are going through a difficult time and feel distant from God. Or we are frustrated by unanswered prayers. Maybe we feel that God isn't acting as we think He should. Sometimes we struggle with doubt and don't even realize it. This occurs when we try to control things or worry. This means that deep down, we don't trust God to handle things for us.

I hope I don't offend anyone, but I am being authentic; I sometimes struggle when I read certain books of the Old Testament (i.e., Leviticus and Exodus). I find it better for my faith not to spend a lot of time reading and trying to analyze these books of the Bible. And I also struggle with and try to over-analyze things like Jonah being in the belly of the fish for three days. However, I do believe that everything is possible with God.

When we have doubts, we can consider ourselves in good company. When Peter first walked on water and began to sink, Jesus said, *"You of little faith, why did you doubt?"* (Matthew 14:31 ESV). Another illustration of doubt comes from Thomas (also known as Doubting Thomas). In John 20:25, after the resurrection, Thomas said, *"unless I see the nail marks in his hands and I put my finger where the nails were and put my hand into his side, I will not believe it."* Talk about doubt; he was looking for some serious validation! When Jesus appeared to Thomas, he said, *"Because you have seen me, you have believed. Blessed are those who have not seen and yet have believed"* (John 20:29 NKJV).

I know that I have gone through long periods of doubt during my walk with Christ. Here are some things that may help when you are having doubts.

Spend some time in nature and examine God's beautiful creation

Take a walk, listen to the birds sing, watch the waves, look at the stars. Think about the miracle of birth. I believe that God speaks of His love, power, and majesty through all He has made.

- *"The heavens declare the glory of God; the skies proclaim the work of his hands"* (Psalm 19:1).

- *"For since the creation of the world God's invisible qualities—his eternal power and divine nature—have been clearly seen, being understood from what has been made, so that men are without excuse"* (Romans 1:20).

Think about all the ways that God has worked in your life

Write them down in a journal and refer to them when you have feelings of doubt.

Read the Bible and other books to strengthen your belief

The Case for Christ and *The Case for Faith*, both by Lee Strobel, are really good reads for those struggling with faith and doubt. These books helped me earlier in my journey when I wasn't sure what I believed.

Ask God for His help

Pray about the feelings of doubt that you are having and ask for the strength to overcome. Turn your doubts into questions and questions into prayers. In Mark 9:14-27, a father who brought his demon-possessed son to Jesus for healing said, *"I do believe; help me overcome my unbelief!"*

Decide to believe and try to put doubts out of your head when they surface

There is controversy on the topic of whether we can decide to believe, but I think we can. I just remind myself that if there isn't a God, there is no hope or salvation. That's an extremely depressing thought, and I don't want to live even one day of my life with that mindset.

Is there a Heaven and a Hell? Does God really exist? I'm not one hundred percent sure, but I truly hope there is. And in my heart, I believe there is. We were never meant to understand everything while we are in this world. Isaiah 55:9 reminds us: *"As the heavens are higher than the earth, so are my ways higher than your ways and my thoughts than your thoughts."* First Corinthians 13:12 says, *"For now we see only a reflection as in a mirror; then we shall see face to face. Now I know in part; then I shall know fully, even as I am fully known."* Until that time, we will always have questions.

In conclusion, there are days when my faith is tested, and I wonder how there can be a God when so many terrible things happen in the world. I still haven't figured out an answer to that question, and I never will while I'm on this earth.

However, I do know that I never feel alone when I pray, and I am filled with a feeling of peace. I truly believe that God is watching over us.

> *"Trust in the Lord with all your heart and lean not on your own understanding; in all your ways submit to him, and he will make your paths straight"* (Proverbs 3:5-6).

<u>REFLECT</u>

- Have you had periods of doubt? Or are you in one now?
- What has helped you to overcome your doubts?
- Think about circumstances where God has worked in your life. Jot these down and reference them as a reminder of Him.

53

The Waiting Is the Hardest Part

"Be completely humble and gentle; be patient, bearing with one another in love" (Ephesians 4:2).

In the words of Tom Petty, "the waiting is the hardest part." In our society, we are conditioned to want and get everything fast. It started with fast food and microwaves. Now you can deposit a check, transfer money from your phone, order something online, and get it the next day. We want instant gratification. However, we all have to deal at times with other people or circumstances that try our patience—an ungrateful child, slow service in a retail store, a long line, a spouse taking us for granted, coworkers who don't pull their weight, the pandemic to end… The list could go on and on.

By nature, I'm not a very patient person. I want what I want, and I want it now! I think I get it from my dad. If we had to wait more than five minutes at a restaurant, we had to go somewhere else. After we went to several "somewhere else's," we could have finished eating at the first restaurant.

God has been working on improving my patience. He gave me Alexis, my oldest daughter. We can be scheduled to be somewhere at five o'clock, and at four fifty-five, she is getting in the shower, and her showers are not short. He also gave me Tracy, my husband, who goes at one pace, and that's pretty slow… His family jokes that he is on "Tracy time." We call him "Clark Griswold" on vacation. He's a ton of fun to wait on in museums. I have whipped through a whole museum and find him still at the first display reading. It is pretty much the same in the grocery store. The other day as I was ready to check out, I found him reading the label on a water bottle. God sure has a sense of humor!

I'm sure that you, like me, have prayed and prayed about issues you are facing, and nothing seems to happen. You just wait. I'm in one of those periods now and feel like I am in that situation much of the time. It's easy to feel like your bank of patience is depleting. That's when I often try to swoop in and take care of the situation instead of trusting God to do so in His timing. And it usually doesn't end well.

We've all heard the quote, "Patience is a virtue." Paul lists patience as part of the fruit of the spirit (Galatians 5:22-23). There's no disputing that Christians are supposed to be patient.

What is patience? Here are a couple of definitions:
- The capacity to accept or tolerate delay, trouble, or suffering without getting angry or upset.
- To suffer without complaining or becoming annoyed.

Jesus is the perfect model of patience. His disciples were sometimes stubborn, lazy, selfish, and doubtful. Despite all they saw Jesus do and say, they focused on themselves and wavered in their belief. Yet, in every interaction, Jesus demonstrated patience. God wants us to be like Him. The more we become Christ-like, the more we will develop patience: for ourselves, our families, our friends, and everything and everyone else. The Bible is full of examples of people that demonstrated patience—Noah, David, and Abraham, to name a few.

Paul teaches us some lessons about patience. In Colossians 3:12, he said that we should put on the virtues of *"compassion, kindness, humility, gentleness, and patience."* In Ephesians 4:2-3, he instructed us to *"be completely humble and gentle; be patient, bearing with one another in love. Make every effort to keep the unity of the Spirit through the bond of peace."*

Below are some tips that can help you to "wait well."

<u>Trials produce patience</u>

Going through trials helps us to become more patient. Think this way: the more trials we face, the more opportunities we get to cultivate patience. James 1:2-4 tells us:

Consider it pure joy, my brothers and sisters, whenever you face trials of many kinds, because you know that the testing of your faith produces perseverance. Let perseverance finish its work so that you may be mature and complete, not lacking anything.

Trials are necessary to grow our faith, our character, and our patience. It's hard for us to see trials as a good thing, but they can surely help us learn, grow, and become more like Christ. I don't know about you but, if everything was always going well for me, without trials and challenges, I likely wouldn't turn to God as much and certainly wouldn't have developed into the person I've become. Trials often also result in us using our experience to teach, support and help others.

<u>Be Thankful</u>

How do we "put on…patience" as Paul instructs us (Colossians 3:12)? He points us to thanksgiving.

Let the peace of Christ rule in your hearts, since as members of one body you were called to peace. And be thankful. Let the work of

> *Christ dwell in you richly as you teach and admonish one another with all wisdom, and as you sing Psalms, hymns and spiritual songs with gratitude in your hearts to God. And whatever you do, whether in word or deed, do it all in the name of the Lord Jesus, giving thanks to God the Father through him (Colossians 3:15-17).*

Okay, we get it, Paul. Thankfulness was mentioned not just once but three times in this passage.

Further, in Colossians 1:11-12 (BSB), Paul prays that we may be:
> *strengthened with all power according to His glorious might so that you may have full endurance and patience, and joyfully giving thanks to the Father, who has qualified you to share in the inheritance of the saints in the light.*

The unwelcome intrusions of waiting into our lives are powerful opportunities to welcome God into every moment, be thankful for Him, and keep our hearts renewed in Him.

Trust God

It is not in our abilities to know the time or way God will work things out. Ecclesiastes 3:11 (BSB) says,
> *He has made everything beautiful in its time. He has also set eternity in the hearts of men; yet they cannot fathom the work that God has done from the beginning to end.*

This is a great reminder that God is in control, and we will never understand everything while we are on this earth. Our role is to trust Him and wait with hope as God brings to completion the good work He has begun in each of our lives.

The next time you are stuck in traffic, frustrated by your spouse, or in a period of waiting, how will you respond? Our natural response is impatience which then leads to stress, anger, and frustration. According to 2 Corinthians 5:17, we are no longer in bondage to a "natural response" because we are new creations in Christ. So let's put on our patience and praise and trust God during our periods of waiting.

REFLECT

- Are you in a period of waiting? What are you waiting for?
- Can you think of examples where trials in your life helped you to develop patience?
- What else has helped you to grow in your ability to be patient?
- What can you do to become better at waiting well?

CONFESSIONS OF A HOT MESS- FROM MESS TO MESSage

54
I Can't Get No Satisfaction

If asked what we want most in life, contentment would likely be somewhere towards the top of the list for most of us. Contentment, or the state of being content, is about peaceful satisfaction. It involves appreciating what you have and where you are in life, rather than wishing things were different. As the song says, many of us "can't get no satisfaction." We want to do too much, have too much, and be too much. We desire what we do not have and believe that we will be satisfied and happy if we have it.

I have spent a large portion of my life feeling discontent with myself and what I have, wishing I had more or different. I don't know why this is. I'm blessed with a nice house, a wonderful family, good friends, and everything I need. Unfortunately, our world breeds discontent, and I'm pretty sure I'm not the only one impacted. We are bombarded with messages that make us think we need more possessions, a better job, the perfect marriage, extravagant vacations, and a whole host of other things to be happy.

True contentment isn't something we find in things, people, or circumstances; it can only be found in Christ. The secret to contentment is very simple and can be summed up in this phrase: *"Trust in the Lord with all your heart"* (Proverbs 3:5 GNT). Contentment involves consciously recognizing and appreciating what God is doing no matter what the circumstances. Paul says it best in Philippians 4:11-13:

> *I am not saying this because I am in need, for I have learned to be content whatever the circumstances. I know what it is to be in need, and I know what it is to have plenty. I have learned the secret of being content in any and every situation, whether well fed or hungry, whether living in plenty or in want. I can do all this through him who gives me strength.*

The things that the world values are not what God values. If we focus our mind on Him and others and get it off ourselves, we are much more likely to experience peace and contentment. The Scriptures below remind us that we should focus on things above and not of this world. We have reviewed these verses in other chapters, but the Bible tells us:

* *"Set your minds on things above, not on earthly things"* (Colossians 3:2).

- *"Do not conform any longer to the pattern of this world, but be transformed by the renewing of your mind" (Romans 12:2).*

Many of us have a bad habit of being futuristic. This involves constantly allowing our mind to run off to the future and resting our happiness on achieving some future state. I feel, in a way, that I missed much of my children growing up by not living in the moment and always thinking about the next thing.

Contentment begins with accepting life as it is in each moment, living in the here and now. Remember when we talked about mindfulness? As a reminder, it is noticing what you are doing, feeling, and thinking when you are actually doing, feeling, and thinking it. Christian mindfulness involves paying attention to God and focusing on His kingdom. It can help us to let go of the need to change things. It can also help us to be more content with the life that God has given us.

Minimalism is a concept that is all about focusing on what matters most and encourages removing that which gets in the way. It is often thought of as pairing down material possessions. Although that's part of it, our schedules and our minds need just as much decluttering. I know my mind could be on an episode of Hoarders. Simplifying our lives could involve giving up things that we don't need, saying no to things that don't fit in with our priorities, and even giving up relationships that tax our positivity and peacefulness. We will explore this more in the next chapter.

Making room for quiet is another strategy that can help facilitate peace and contentment. Pray, meditate, spend time in nature or just sit quietly—whatever works for you. These practices help you become better connected with yourself and with God. Try to give up control and release yourself to thoughts and emotions that can heal and strengthen you and produce feelings of peace and contentment.

Jesus described the kind of experience he wants us to have in our lives:
Therefore I tell you, do not worry about your life, what you will eat; or about your body, what you will wear... For the pagan world runs after all such things, and your Father knows that you need them. But seek his kingdom, and these things will be given to you as well (Luke 12:22, 30-31).

REFLECT

- When have you felt most content in your life? What stage of life were you in? What were you doing?
- Think about how you get more of that and what changes you can make to experience more contentment in your life.

55

A Simpler Life

Does your life feel overly complicated? Does it feel like you are pulled in a dozen different directions? Do you ever wish for a quieter, simpler time, like Little House on the Prairie? No cell phones, no checking email at night, no "taxi service" for the kids, less drama. Of course, lack of electricity might be a problem... And I'm pretty sure I would have to cook and sew, which would definitely be a problem. But a simple life sounds pretty good to me at this juncture. I am envisioning a log cabin in the mountains. But I would need to be fairly close to shopping, Starbucks, and Wi-Fi.

Jesus lived a really simple lifestyle. He traveled to teach and heal without much baggage. He ate and stayed at other people's homes and encouraged his disciples to do the same (Mark 10:10). He was focused on one thing and one thing only—spreading the Word of God.

Jesus says, *"I came that they may have life and have it abundantly"* (*John 10:10 ESV*). The life that he speaks of is not about fortune, fame, or material possessions. It is a life rich in love (of God and other people) where we are doing God's work. To do this, we have to cut through the clutter in our lives, ditch unimportant things, and manage the complications.

Even in a world full of distractions and many shiny things that catch our attention, it's possible to live a focused, simple life. We have to let go of things that hinder our walk with God, freeing ourselves up to live a life of commitment to Him. This will also help to increase our contentment in our lives.

If your life feels complicated and out of control, choose to take it to its simplest form. Here are some tips to consider:

- Learn to live with what you need and within your means
- Take a break from social media and technology
- Spend time in nature
- Don't try to be more or less than God's design for you
- Spend time with people you enjoy and decrease or eliminate time

spent with toxic people

- Love and spend quality time with your family
- Own what you actually need and make it simple to care for
- Keep an eternal focus

Easy peasy, right? Maybe not that easy, but you can consider baby steps in this direction. I'm getting ready to go through my closet. I probably really don't need fifteen pairs of boots. Note to Marie Kondo: They do bring me joy!

> *"…and make it your ambition to lead a quiet life: You should mind your own business and work with your hands, just as we told you"* (1 Thessalonians 4:11).

REFLECT

- What will you do to simplify your life?

56

Don't Be a Debbie Downer

"As I have observed, those who plow evil and those who sow trouble reap it" (Job 4:80).

Some people wake up in the morning with an attitude of gratitude. Others wake up with a sense of dread, worry, and lack of joy. I typically wake up feeling a little negative, grumpy, and tired–coffee helps, though. Those that wake up all perky and happy get on my nerves. But I do wish I could be that way.

Debbie Downer is one of my favorite characters on Saturday Night Live. If you aren't familiar, she is always bringing others down with random negative comments. In my favorite episode, she was with a group talking about how excited they were after their first day at Disneyland. Debbie inserted negative comments throughout the conversation and ended with the announcement that her cat had feline AIDS. It doesn't sound that funny, but it is–not that feline AIDS is funny. We all have negative people in our lives that drain our energy and optimism. It can be exhausting. And we may even be that person from time to time!

Negativity is a natural human response. And let's face it, there are many things going on in the world that can cause us to go negative. Just watching the news can do it for me! Our brains are wired to notice threats, problems, and setbacks so that we can protect ourselves from what is bad. Because of this, we have to work extra hard to stay positive.

One way that we show negativity is through complaining. I participated in a seven-day no complaining challenge at work, and I didn't even make it through the morning on the first day. I don't think we realize how much we complain. I know I didn't until I was making a conscious effort not to.

God desires for us to have a positive perspective and see our lives as overflowing with His love, grace, joy, and peace. When we are negative, we aren't believing God's promises and are limiting our reliance on Him. First Timothy 4:12 tells us to *"set an example for the believers in speech, in conduct, in love, in faith and in purity."*

Below are some ways that we can demonstrate positivity and fight off negative tendencies.

Practice Gratitude

Have you noticed that this is a theme throughout these lessons? We are told to be thankful numerous times in the Psalms (Psalms 30:4; 50:14; 92:1; 95:2; 100:4; 105:1; 136:6; etc.). In 1 Thessalonians, Paul tells us that thanksgiving is a part of God's will for each one of us. One simple way to overcome negativity is to practice gratitude. Research shows that when we count three blessings a day, we get a measurable boost in happiness that uplifts and energizes us. It's also physiologically impossible to be stressed and thankful at the same time as two thoughts cannot occupy our minds concurrently. Ephesians 5:20 tell us to always give thanks to God the Father for everything, in the name of our Lord Jesus Christ.

Look at what's going right - Rather than what's going wrong

We tend to focus on things that aren't going well. Try to shift and keep your eyes and ears open for things that are going well. Instead of complaining about what others are doing wrong, focus on what they are doing right. Praise them and tell them that you appreciate them.

Pray

Scientific research shows that daily prayer reduces stress, boosts positive energy, and promotes health and vitality. When you are faced with negative feelings, talk to God and ask him to help you recharge.

It is understandable when those who do not know Christ are negative because they have no hope of anything beyond this world. Negativity in a Christian's attitude means that he or she is refusing to see life from God's perspective. As Christians, we need to exhibit positive energy and offer light in the darkness for others. *"You are the light of the world. A city on a hill cannot be hidden"* (Matthew 5:13 BSB).

REFLECT

- Do you demonstrate negativity in your life? If so, in what areas?
- Practice gratitude by writing down three things each day that you are grateful for.
- If you aren't already, how will you demonstrate more positive energy in your life (at work and home)?

Confessions of a Hot Mess- from MESS to MESSage

57
Battling Body Image

"For you created my inmost being; you knit me together in my mother's womb. I praise you because I am fearfully and wonderfully made; your works are wonderful, I know that full well" (Psalm 139:13-14).

Body image is an issue that almost everybody deals with at some point. Many women, in particular, have an unhealthy view of their bodies which negatively impacts their lives. How many women have you known that have tried fad diets like the lemonade diet, the grapefruit diet, and the military diet? There was even a vision diet where you eat everything with blue-tinted glasses. And there was a thing where you could get a staple in your ear which was supposed to curb your appetite. We'll try just about anything to get the body we want!

Consider these statistics:
- Forty to sixty percent of elementary school girls (ages six to twelve) are concerned about their weight or becoming too fat. This concern endures through life. (https://www.nationaleatingdisorders.org/what-are-eating-disorders)
- The main contributor to the development of eating disorders is body dissatisfaction. In the United States, two million women suffer from a clinically significant eating disorder at some time in their life. (https://www.nationaleatingdisorders.org/what-are-eating-disorders)
- Only two percent of women globally consider themselves beautiful. And two-thirds of women strongly agree that "media and advertising set an unrealistic standard of beauty that most women can't ever achieve." (https://www.dove.com/us/en/stories/about-dove.html)
- A study found that while "fat talk" tended to decrease with age, "old talk" often came in to replace it and that both were reported by women who appeared to have a negative body image. Guilty! (https://www.nytimes.com/2013/02/28/booming/old-talk-and-fat-talk-among-baby-boomers.html)

Confessions of a Hot Mess- from MESS to MESSage

I have had an unhealthy relationship with body image since my early college years. I started smoking in high school and, by my sophomore year in college, I decided to quit. I heard that many people who quit smoking gain weight, and I was worried about that. I believe that to be what started my unhealthy obsession with being thin. I started doing cardio and lifting weights and was very conscious of what I ate. The thing back then was "low-fat," so I ate low-fat everything. Occasionally, I would binge on something and then have terrible feelings of guilt and exercise extra hard the next day. By the end of my senior year of college, I was down to ninety-nine pounds which wasn't a healthy weight for my five-foot-five-inch frame.

I continued to struggle as I got older. One of my roles in a previous job was to lead employee wellness efforts at my organization. Although this was right up my alley, I think it made me even a little more obsessive about health and fitness. I tried to impose my diet choices on my family, and shockingly they were pretty resistant. My husband eats like a middle school boy, and my daughters wanted stuff they thought tasted good, like french fries and chicken nuggets. In addition, I tried to get everyone to exercise and was a failure there as well. I don't think my daughters have ever been as mad at me as when I signed them up for a personal training session in middle school, and the trainer had them doing jump squats and burpees.

Admittedly, I still struggle with my body image. I exercise every day with few exceptions and try to make healthy food choices. I still experience anxiety at times if I make unhealthy food choices or don't find time to exercise.

In Genesis 3, Eve was tempted by Satan. Does anyone else find it ironic that the first temptation involved food? I might have been more tempted by doughnuts or pizza than an apple, though. Just sayin'.

Genesis 1:27 tells us that God created us in His image. Isn't that amazing? We are made in the image of the most flawless, perfect being ever to exist! Our body is our temporary dwelling place while we are on this earth. Although I believe that we should be good stewards of our bodies, it doesn't determine our worth. God thinks we are beautiful just the way we are. Even with stretch marks. Even with a muffin top. And even with bat wings. Reminding yourself of this can help you to prevail in the battle of body image.

Below are some tips to try to work on your body image:
- Stop letting the number on the scale define you.
- Pray and ask God to help you let go of your negative body image issues.
- Pay attention to your body and what it needs. Honor God by treating your body with love and respect and nourish it well.

REFLECT

- Do you battle with your body image?
- What will you do to work on improving your body image?

58

Mirror, Mirror on the Wall

Remember "Mirror, mirror on the wall, who's the fairest of them all" from Snow White? Most of us became familiar with this when we were kids. And sadly, that's when many of us began to think that "happily ever after's" were only for beautiful people. Our culture seems to be obsessed with physical appearance. And, for most of us women, we feel pressure to be beautiful. We see images of women representing the ideal of beauty—skinny, beautiful hair and eyes, white teeth, stylish clothes, and a thigh gap, to name a few. What's up with the thigh gap thing anyway?

From the time that we were little girls, most of us desired to be beautiful. I remember hating my nose and trying to pull on it to make it longer and pointier. Didn't work. And I remember wishing I was more "blessed"—you know what I mean. Now it's fine with me as I don't have a sagging problem.

Unfortunately, we live in a superficial world where people do judge on appearance. We would all love to say that we are not in the majority and that we look beyond what's on the outside, but virtually all of us are influenced by the appearance of others.

There is some value placed on physical beauty in the Bible. Sarah, Rebekah, and Rachel are all described as beautiful. But here are a few reminders from Proverbs that godly character matters far more than beauty.

- *"Like a gold ring in a pig's snout is a beautiful woman who shows no discretion" (Proverbs 11:22).*

- *"Charm is deceptive and beauty is fleeting; but a woman who fears the Lord is to be praised" (Proverbs 31:30 BSB).*

As we all know and the verse above indicates, outward beauty fades as we age. I was never close to being a ten, but I'm way down on the scale now. As we get older, wrinkles, gray hair, sun spots, waddles, and even chin hair (or maybe that's just me) appear. Some women resort to Botox, plastic surgery, facial treatments, liposuction—whatever it takes to maintain their outward appearance. I am choosing to see these imperfections as battle scars that I have earned over the years.

In 1 Peter 3:3-4, the Apostle Peter states that Christians should not focus on outward beauty but on inner beauty:

> Your beauty should not come from outward adornment, such as elaborate hairstyles and the wearing of gold jewelry and fine clothes. Rather, it should be that of your inner self, the unfading beauty of a gentle and quiet spirit, which is of great worth in God's sight.

First Samuel 16:7 (ESV) further emphasizes this point: "...*the Lord sees not as man sees: man looks on the outward appearance, but the Lord looks on the heart.*"

So, should Christians care about physical appearance? I believe that the answer is "yes," but with a strong caveat that our reason for caring should be that we want to please God with our bodies. There is nothing wrong with making the best of what God has given us as long as we don't become obsessive about it. If the reason we try to be the perfect weight, wear fashionable clothes, have facials, etc., is to impress other people, then our physical appearance has become a matter of pride. So, we need to keep appearance in perspective. The Bible encourages us to present ourselves as nicely as possible, but God does not call us to go to extremes. We must be aware of why we do the things we do to maintain or enhance our physical appearance.

Ask yourself the question, "Are you more focused on your appearance than you are on God?" If you answered "yes," you may need to examine your priorities. We should be more focused on our hearts and actions rather than our image and appearance. And there are some aspects of our appearance that we just can't change. We need to accept that God made us the way he did for a reason and that He knows what he is doing. We are *"fearfully and wonderfully made" (Psalm 139:14)*.

REFLECT

- Do you have a healthy relationship with your outward appearance—or are you overly focused on it?
- What will you do to keep this in check?

_____
_____
_____
_____
_____
_____
_____

59

Wrinkles and Blemishes

"...and to present her to himself as a radiant church, without stain or wrinkle or any other blemish, but holy and blameless" (Ephesians 5:27).

When my stepdaughter has a zit (blemish), she calls it a "Helga." We send each other pictures of our "Helga's." Kind of gross, I know, but that's how we roll. Now I don't know why she chose that name, and I apologize to any Helga's who might be reading this.

I don't get as many zits as I used to, but the zits have been replaced with many other imperfections. As I mentioned in the last chapter, I am now overrun with wrinkles, age spots, and an occasional chin hair. Even the women considered the most beautiful in my younger days (i.e., Cindy Crawford, Julia Roberts) are affected by the imperfections that come with the aging process. Jennifer Aniston is an enigma, though. I chalk it up to not having kids.

To be without blemish is to be without a mark, problem, or imperfection. I don't know about you, but I have all of these! I don't believe that this refers to our physical imperfections but the blemishes and imperfections within our hearts. It is God's desire for us to one day appear before Him holy and blameless–with a clean heart! Mark 7:20-23 (BSB) says,

> *What comes out of a man, that is what defiles him. For from within the hearts of men come evil thoughts, sexual immorality, theft, murder, adultery, greed, deceit, debauchery, envy, slander, arrogance and foolishness. All these evils come from within, and these are what defile a man.*

This is quite the list of things that come out of us! Some things are obvious– we know that murder and adultery are unclean acts. But this list includes less obvious sins like arrogance, envy, and greed. So, how do we cultivate a clean heart? I believe that we follow Jesus' example and try to avoid the things listed that make us unclean. Will we likely backslide? We are human and will most definitely run into problems from time to time. When we do, we can review this list and get ourselves back on track.

Someday, we will present ourselves to God in all of our glory. He already thinks we are beautiful. However, no matter how physically attractive we may be, we all have stains, wrinkles, and blemishes to contend with. The best we can do is to follow His example and work towards a clean heart.

> *Create in me a clean heart, O God, and renew a right spirit within me. Cast me not away from your presence, and take not your Holy Spirit from me. Restore to me the joy of your salvation, and uphold me with a willing spirit"* (Psalm 51:10-12 ESV).

REFLECT

- What blemishes or imperfections do you struggle with the most?
- What can you do to work towards a clean heart?

60

Proverbs 31 Woman vs. Hot Mess

The Proverbs 31 woman is the Wonder Woman of the Bible. She annoyingly conquers life with little or no difficulty. She is a woman of virtue and character.

As I began writing to compare and contrast "hot mess" (me) with this virtuous woman, I thought—this is going to be a bloodbath. First of all, I'm not that "womanly." I pretty much suck at many traditional things in which women often excel—cooking, cleaning, gardening, sewing, crafts. And my husband keeps asking me when I'm going to write about being a submissive wife. God has some more work to do on me for sure before I can get there. I tend to want to run things in our relationship.

Take some time to read Proverbs 31. What an amazing woman! Admittedly, she sets a seemingly impossible standard for us to meet. Do you know any women that exhibit all of these characteristics? Or anyone even close? Thank goodness this isn't designed to be a "checklist for women," as I think most of us would not get a good report.

Some of the verses are a little dated where it talks about distaffs, spindles, and such. Here's how I picture the modern-day Proverbs 31 woman:

She is very well put together, well dressed, and physically fit with killer arms. She has a high-powered, successful career while also managing to be a great mom. She is very faithful. She is highly involved in her church and volunteers at the homeless shelter regularly. Her children are always well pressed and well-behaved. She cooks tasty, healthy meals for her family, and her home is always immaculate. She is a good steward of her family's money and always gets the best values on really nice things. And she is always even-keeled and never loses her cool. I don't like her much…

Let's break it down and look at some of the traits of the Proverbs 31 woman:

1. **She is faithful.** *"…but a woman who fears the Lord is to be praised" (Proverbs 31:30).* First and foremost, she is faithful and always puts God first in her life. She loves and serves Him with her heart, mind, and soul. She seeks his will and follows his ways.

2. **She is a good wife.** *"Her husband has full confidence in her and lacks*

nothing of value. She brings him good, not harm, all the days of her life" (Proverbs 31:12). She respects her husband. He can trust her to make wise choices and behave with wisdom. She is an asset to him and does good things for him every day.

3. **She is a hard worker.** *"...and works with eager hands"* (Proverbs 31:13). *"She sets about her work vigorously; her arms are strong for her task"* (Proverbs 31:17). She is eager to work and has a diligent work ethic. She never slacks off and is always productive.

4. **She is a good mother.** *"Her children arise and call her blessed"* (Proverbs 31:28). She teaches her children the ways of God, nurtures them with love, and trains them up in the way they should go.

5. **She is a wise steward.** *"She considers a field and buys it; out of her earnings she plants a vineyard"* (Proverbs 31:16). She spends money wisely and is careful to purchase quality items that her family needs.

6. **She is generous.** *"She opens her arms to the poor and extends her hands to the needy"* (Proverbs 31:20). She is aware of the needs of others around her and reaches out to help them.

7. **She is strong and dignified.** *"She is clothed with strength and dignity, She laughs at the time to come"* (Proverbs 31:25). She is courageous and has control over her emotions. She is dignified, which means she carries herself well and has earned the respect of others.

8. **She embraces beauty.** *"She makes coverings for her bed; She is clothed in fine linen and purple"* (Proverbs 31:22). She takes good care of herself. Her beauty isn't just on the outside; she also has an inner beauty that comes from Christ. She uses her creativity and style to create beauty in her life and the lives of others.

9. **She is an industrious businesswoman.** *"She sees that her trading is profitable, and her lamp does not go out at night"* (Proverbs 31:18). *"She makes linen garments and sells them, and supplies the merchants with sashes"* (Proverbs 31:24). She adds to her family's wealth by using her talents.

10. **She watches her words.** *"She speaks with wisdom, And faithful instruction is on her tongue"* (Proverbs 31:26). She knows when it is a good idea to speak and when to hold her tongue.

I won't share all of the ways that I differ from the Proverbs 31 woman. Suffice it to say, this would be a lengthy chapter if I did. Here are a few things that don't match up:

- I'm not very good at working with "eager hands" around the house.

This brings to mind a woman preparing dinner with a smile and singing while she cleans the house. Nope—not me. A Proverbs 31 woman also doesn't grumble while completing her tasks. I remember stomping around the house loudly when I would cook or clean, mad because others weren't helping. Of course, no one seemed to notice or care.

* I'm also not the best at being a good steward. I thoroughly enjoy shopping which certainly takes away from stewardship. I continue to work to have better self-control, particularly when it comes to buying clothes and shoes.

* I'm certainly not going to be making any bed coverings or linen garments. You could tell that from my earlier comments!

* I don't think I'm always the best wife. I don't do good things for my husband EVERY day, as it says in the passage. I could certainly be more attentive and engaged with him. Also, my children certainly don't rise and call me blessed. I have had my share of parenting fails.

The good news is that, although I don't measure up, I feel that I at least possess some of the traits listed. I try to be the best wife and mother I can be, although I know I frequently fall short. And I strive to exhibit many of the other characteristics on a regular basis. I have certainly been working diligently on my faith and cultivating a deeper relationship with the Lord. The best news of all is that the Proverbs 31 woman was not an actual woman! In this Scripture, King Lemuel's mother was describing the kind of woman she hoped her son would marry.

Most of us will never check off all the boxes to attain the perfection of the virtuous woman. However, we can study the virtues described and strive to live a life where they are evident. We can live out God's will for our lives and live each day with purpose, always determined to be the best woman we can be.

REFLECT

* What are some areas where you fall short of the Proverbs 31 woman that you would like to work on?

* What actions can you take to be the best woman you can be?

_____
_____
_____
_____

Leslie Speas

61
Abnormal Is Better Than Normal

My family isn't normal. Probably not a surprise since I write about being a hot mess. Some of that probably rubs off, right? Or maybe they contributed to my hot mess status. The latest news is that my daughter got a Morticia tattoo. She is in divinity school, and I'm sure that will be a plus for her to get a job in ministry. It has been said that "she will be able to minister to people that look like her." I hope the Adams family is in the market for a minister—and Pippi Longstocking because she has dyed her hair orange. In all seriousness, I am very proud of her. She obviously doesn't seem to care what others think of her. She is also very smart, and I'm sure that she will make a difference in the world. She calls girls that look more normal "basic." A little more basic would be okay with me, but whatever.

My oldest daughter is definitely hot mess junior. She has always been a little different. She is obsessed with names and family blogs. She has also been known to be a bit of a "stalker" on social media. I think she is just interested and likes to know stuff about people, but it's a little creepy. She has had a hard time as of late, so I will mention her only minimally here. But my younger daughter said when she was leaving for college that she would "crash and burn." And she kind of did, although thankfully, she is pulling it together now.

My step-daughter got married, and we didn't find out until afterward, right before it hit Facebook. My other step-daughter just got engaged. Thankfully, she let us know. When asked what kind of wedding she wanted, she said a wedding in the woods. We are okay with it; sounds inexpensive.

My father is highly intelligent and is a retired Radiological Physicist. He has the sense of humor of a middle school boy. When I was a teenager, he put a bag over his head like the unknown comic—only those of a certain age will understand that—and came out on the beach where I was sunbathing, trying to impress the lifeguard. Just one example of the many things he has done in my life to embarrass me. He calls it sensitivity training. My mother has passed away, but she had a very dark sense of humor. She was probably the only 80-year-old in the world that enjoyed *Trailer Park Boys* and *It's Always Sunny in Philadelphia*.

My brother has made me promise to never write about him, but suffice it to say that he is a character. I can maybe get away with sharing one from when he was little. He would tell people to "smell his foot" and stick his foot up in the air at strangers. Today, his cats have Facebook pages and are pretty active posters. I will leave my husband out of it, but there are some stories there too.

Now that I have thrown everyone under the bus, let's explore the concept of "normal." What is normal? Who determines what normal is? If you look up normal in any English dictionary, the definition is "usual, regular, common, typical." Normal people are content with routines, patterns, and societal norms. Typically, they are not very deep or creative. Normal people are judgmental of anything that deviates from their rules of normality. How did this become something to aspire to be? How did everyone being the same achieve the cultural push it has?

Abnormal is defined as the opposite of that which is typical or expected; unusual, or exceptional. I don't know about you, but that actually sounds a lot better than normal to me! John the Baptist certainly wasn't normal. He is described as wearing clothes of camel's hair, living on locusts and wild honey. But John was clearly special. He later baptized Jesus. And what about Noah? People probably thought he was nuts for building an ark, and I'm sure he got ridiculed a time or two. He certainly showed them!

Saul was an impressive dude by the world's standards. He came from a God-fearing family, he was a Pharisee like his father, and he was educated by a respected rabbi. I'm sure people thought he had lost his mind when he did an about-face and started following Jesus. But he turned out to be one of the most influential leaders of the early Christian church.

The moral of this story is that being normal isn't all that it is cracked up to be. Whew, what a relief!

REFLECT

- What is odd or unique about your family, and how is that a good thing?

_____
_____
_____
_____
_____
_____
_____
_____

Leslie Speas

Section 5:

SOS
(Strength Out of Struggles)

LESLIE SPEAS

62

Avoiding Temptation

"Blessed is the man who perseveres under trial, because when he has stood the test, he will receive the crown of life that God has promised to those who love him" (James 1:12 BSB).

Dictionary.com defines temptation as the desire to do something, especially something wrong or unwise. I don't know about you, but for me, daily life involves a continual battle with temptation. I worry. I envy. I lust. I try to control. I am prideful.

There was a time in my life when I was in a difficult marriage where I was tempted to be unfaithful. I was getting attention from someone who was being friendly and thoughtful, and I surely didn't have that in my marriage. I thank God I resisted this temptation, but this made me see how easy it could be to give in.

What are the sources of temptation? There are three—the world, the flesh, and Satan.

- **The World-** The world doesn't value what God values. The world values things such as achievement, success, power, beauty, approval of others, and sex. It's easy to fall into the trap of "conforming to the standards of this world." We tend to often focus on what is seen rather than what is unseen and try to fill and satisfy ourselves with that which is of this world.

- **The Flesh-** In Romans 7:14-24, Paul said that there was something in the members of his body that he called his flesh, which produced difficulty in his Christian life and made him a prisoner of sin. The flesh is the part of us that is rebellious and does not want to be told what to do. There is a constant struggle between the flesh (where we seek to please ourselves) and our desire to please God. How does the flesh manifest itself in us? According to Paul,

    The acts of the sinful nature are obvious: sexual immorality, impurity and debauchery; idolatry and witchcraft; hatred, discord, jealousy, fits of rage, selfish ambition, dissensions, factions and envy; drunkenness, orgies and the like. I warn you, as I did before, that those who live like this will not inherit the kingdom of God (Galatians 5:19-21).

- **Satan-** Satan can tempt, taunt, and trouble believers by putting ideas, thoughts, and doubts in our minds. He watches to see where we struggle and uses our struggles, along with past hurts and failures, against us. He tries to break the hold the Word of God has on us by taking what God has declared and casting doubt on it. When Satan tempted Eve to do what God had forbidden, he put doubts in her mind. Then he appealed to her desires, tempting her by saying that she and Adam could be like gods.

Satan tempted Jesus in the wilderness for forty days and forty nights. Satan sought to appeal to Jesus' divinity and humanity, and of course, Jesus was strong and didn't give in. I'm sorry to say, but I'm pretty sure that I would have given in immediately to the offer of bread after fasting for forty days and forty nights. I can't even pass up bread when I go out to eat!

First Peter 5:8 tells us:
Be self-controlled and alert. Your enemy the devil prowls around like a roaring lion looking for someone to devour. Resist him, standing firm in the faith, because you know that your brothers throughout the world are undergoing the same kind of sufferings.

We have learned about temptation and where it comes from. How can we resist it?

Submit yourself to God

The best recourse for temptation is to *"Submit yourselves, then, to God. Resist the devil, and he will flee from you"* (James 4:7).

Avoid tempting situations and places

Temptation often comes when you find yourself in certain situations or places. When you recognize one of those situations, it is time to get as far from it as possible. If you are overcoming addiction, don't go to places or hang out with people that might tempt you with drugs or alcohol. If you are tempted to be unfaithful to your spouse, stay away from people or situations that could result in temptation. In 2 Timothy 2:22, Paul told his young friend, Timothy, to *"Flee the evil desires of youth and pursue righteousness, faith, love and peace, along with those who call on the Lord out of a pure heart."*

Fill your mind with good things

Also, remember that our thoughts are as important as our actions, so try not to entertain tempting thoughts. Avoid anything that fills your mind with sinful thoughts and fill it instead with good things by studying God's Word and praying for His guidance. Many verses in Scripture will help you overcome certain temptations. Committing Bible verses to memory to help combat your areas of temptation can provide good protection and defense.

Confess and repent

If you succumb to temptation, confess, and repent. Ask God to help you stay strong in the future!

REFLECT

- In what areas of your life are you experiencing temptation?
- What will you do to help you avoid these areas of temptation?

_____
_____
_____
_____
_____
_____
_____
_____
_____
_____
_____
_____
_____
_____
_____
_____
_____
_____
_____
_____
_____
_____

63

Practicing Self-Control

"Like a city whose walls are broken through is a person who lacks self-control" (Proverbs 25:28).

Self-control involves delaying an impulse or gratification for a greater purpose or cause. When we exercise self-control, we are saying "no" for the sake of a greater "yes." Self-control isn't easy. If more people demonstrated it, the prisons, hospitals, and courts would have a lot less business!

I can fairly easily exercise self-control as it relates to some things. However, I struggle where it involves chocolate, coffee, wine, shopping, and sometimes my mouth (meaning what comes out of it). Full disclosure here, I really like wine. I got to a place where I was having a glass of wine often as my chill-down time, and it wasn't necessarily the recommended serving size. I have been praying about the things where I lack self-control, and recently two of my favorite boutiques closed. If wineries and coffee shops start shutting down, I may be to blame!

I am also pretty good at justifying my lack of self-control. I justify overindulging in shopping by telling myself things like, "Well, we could need a new roof, and we don't." I also tell myself things like, "I've had a rough day and deserve to have that chocolate bar or glass of wine."

Does God care if I exercise self-control as it relates to these types of things? I think He must, or they wouldn't be on my mind as things that I should better control! Sometimes I think that he has us put self-control to work in everyday things to be ready to better exercise our self-control muscles in the spiritual race ahead of us.

If we want to be successful as Christians, we need to cultivate self-control. It is mentioned as one of the fruits of the spirit in Galatians 5:22 (ESV): *"But the fruit of the Spirit is love, joy, peace, patience, kindness, goodness, faithfulness, gentleness and self-control."*

There might be a reason that it is the last fruit of Spirit listed as it is likely the hardest to master. Self-control requires spiritual maturity and reliance on God to help us garner the strength to deny ourselves.

Jesus is probably the only person who ever demonstrated perfect self-control throughout his life. The Bible says he had no sin (2 Corinthians 5:21). Think about all of the self-control he had to muster to have no sin! Especially when Satan tempted him in the wilderness.

In Matthew 16:24 (ESV), Jesus told his disciples, *"If anyone would come after me, let him deny himself and take up his cross and follow me."* I think this means that we must "take up our cross" in our thoughts. When thoughts that aren't pleasing to God come to our minds, we should put them to death on an inner cross, thus exercising self-control.

We are tempted by things of this world every day. Once we give in and Satan gets a stronghold in one area of our lives, he will work as hard as he can for his influence to bleed into other areas of our lives.

> *For everything in the world—the cravings of sinful man, the lust of his eyes and the boasting of what he has and does—comes not from the Father but from the world. The world and its desires pass away, but the man who does the will of God lives forever (1 John 2:16-17).*

Matthew 5:29 (BSB) says: *"If your right eye causes you to sin, gouge it out and throw it away. It is better for you to lose one part of your body than for your whole body to be thrown into hell."* No thank you, don't want to lose any body parts! But we should examine our lives for anything that causes us to sin and take any action needed to remove it immediately. And exercise self-control to make sure it doesn't happen again!

To develop self-control, we must recognize our weaknesses. Some of us are tempted by binging on food and/or drink, others by gambling, others by shopping, others by sex–the list could go on and on. If we are aware of our temptations, we will be able to take our struggles to God and ask for His help in overcoming them.

What if you fail in your quest to demonstrate self-control? Unfortunately, we are likely to fail at times. Ask for forgiveness from God, forgive yourself, and move on!

> *"So prepare your minds for action and exercise self-control. Put all your hope in the gracious salvation that will come to you when Jesus Christ is revealed to the world"* (1 Peter 1:13 NLT).

REFLECT

- What is one area of your life where you are succeeding in exercising self-control?

- What is one area where you would like to exercise more self-control? What will you do to achieve this?

64

Rejecting Rejection

"The Lord makes firm the steps of the one who delights in him; though he may stumble, he will not fall, for the Lord upholds him with his hand" (Psalm 37:23-24).

Have you ever felt left out and rejected? I know I have. If you haven't, you are a very lucky individual. Here's a few examples of my rejections:

- When I was a kid, I absolutely hated it when we would pick teams in gym class as I was not very athletic and was frequently one of the last ones picked.
- There were times when I wasn't invited to that birthday or slumber party.
- My parents divorced when I was in my early teens, and I felt rejected as if I wasn't worth staying for.
- In high school, I was on the fringes of the popular crowd and never really felt "good enough" or fully accepted.
- I have been through two job eliminations. Even though neither of these was personal, it was hard not to feel rejected.
- I had a failed marriage, and a lot of pain and feelings of rejection were involved.
- As with many of us, I have experienced my share of rejection through breakups or betrayal from others, where it hurt so bad that it seemed like life would never be the same.

I'm not putting these things out there to have a pity party. I know that many people have experienced much worse! I love to listen to podcasts and read books by Joyce Meyer, a Christian author and speaker. Joyce was sexually abused by her father for many years and speaks of this often in her teaching. I can't even imagine how you rebound from that—except with God!

Social media certainly hasn't helped us with our feelings of rejection. We can easily scroll and see pictures of friends doing things together, and we were not invited. People often say hurtful things via social media, contributing to negative emotions. As difficult of a time as I had with feelings of rejection in middle school and high school, I can't even imagine how much it has escalated for kids today with the addition of technology.

Rejection is hurtful but, unfortunately, is a part of life. In the book, *Uninvited: Living Loved When You Feel Less Than, Left Out and Lonely*, LysaTerKeurst says:
> Rejection isn't just an emotion we feel. It's a message that's sent to the core of who we are, causing us to believe lies about ourselves, others, and God. Rejection then can become a liability in how we think about ourselves and interact in future relationships.

The word "rejection" comes from the Latin noun rēicere, which means "to throw back." When we experience rejection, it often stops us in our tracks and causes us to retreat. As I mentioned before, I love Brené Brown's work on vulnerability. Her research shows that the willingness to be vulnerable is essential to building trusting relationships and living our best lives. If we aren't willing to be vulnerable because we fear rejection, we won't be willing to put ourselves out there and live out the purpose for our lives that God has for us.

Jesus was surely not immune to rejection. From the onset of his ministry, he was rejected by the Pharisees, the Jews, and even his friends, who said they loved and would never leave him. With each rejection Jesus faced, he kept moving forward towards his goal. His greatest agony was when God turned away from him on the cross. When I think about this, I feel bad that I have struggled so much with the small amount of rejection I have faced when Jesus suffered the worst rejection ever for us.

We live in a broken world where rejection is sure to happen. In John 15:18, Jesus told his disciples to expect rejection. "If the world hates you, keep in mind that it hated me first."

Here are some things that you can do to help overcome the sting of rejection:
- Realize that people who reject you are definitely in the minority. When you think about all of the people you have encountered in your life, there is probably only a very small percentage that has ever seriously rejected you.

- Acknowledge your emotions and how you are feeling. If you deny or "stuff" your feelings, it's only going to make you feel worse in the long run.

- View rejection as evidence that you were courageous and stepped outside your comfort zone to do something.

- Don't let rejection define you! You shouldn't let your self-worth be based on other people's opinions of you. Remember who you are in God.

- Realize that God may have something better for you or be protecting you from something through the rejection.
- Use the experience as an opportunity to examine your situation and determine ways to learn, grow, and/or help others. For example, rejection for a job could become a motivation to further your education. Or a spouse leaving you could result in an opportunity to help others going through similar situations.
- Reflect on Scriptures that will uplift you when you are feeling rejected.
    - *"The Lord makes firm the steps of the one who delights in him; though he may stumble, he will not fall, for the Lord upholds him with his hand" (Psalm 37:23-24).*
    - *"The Lord is close to the brokenhearted and saves those who are crushed in spirit" (Psalm 34:18).*

Remember that God loves and accepts you despite any flaws and insecurities. Try to take your focus off of the rejection and focus on Jesus, your ultimate approver. Realize that feelings of rejection are only temporary. Nothing lasts forever except His love. He will help you through each situation and likely has something better for you as a result!

REFLECT

- Are past rejections impacting your life currently?
- What will you do to try to move past these feelings of rejection and move forward with your life?

_____
_____
_____
_____
_____
_____
_____
_____
_____
_____

65

Define or Refine?

"In this world you will have trouble. But take heart! I have overcome the world" (John 16:33).

Have you ever felt like your life is one struggle after another? Do you wonder if others are going through similar struggles in their lives? Even those who appear to have perfect lives on social media are likely experiencing struggles. We all have them.

- Even the homecoming queen from high school who is still beautiful and seems to have the perfect husband, the perfect house, and the perfect kids.
- Even the celebrity who is admired by many and who has more money than she knows what to do with.
- Even the woman who seems to be able to perfectly balance career success, a family, and everything else in her life.

When struggles come (and they will), we have two options. We can let them define or refine us. When we allow our struggles to define us, we expend a lot of energy feeling sorry for ourselves and wallowing in a victim mentality. And we try to figure out who is to blame or beat ourselves up. When we do this, we stay mired in adversity, and we can't move forward in a positive way.

The other (and preferred) choice is to let the struggle refine us and become better and stronger as a result. We can learn and grow from our struggles. We might even be able to help others as a result, using our pain as our platform.

First Peter 4:12-13 says,

> *Dear friends, do not be surprised at the painful trial you are suffering, as though something strange were happening to you. But rejoice that you participate in the sufferings of Christ, so that you may be overjoyed when his glory is revealed.*

When we experience struggles:
- We can rely on God to comfort us. Have you ever noticed that we

tend to turn away from God when things are going well? Struggles help us get closer to Him, depend on Him, and even help us learn to be more like Him.

> *When you pass through the waters, I will be with you; and when you pass through the rivers, they will not sweep over you. When you walk through the fire, you will not be burned; the flame will not set you ablaze (Isaiah 43:2).*

- Instead of asking "Why, God?", ask the question, "What do you want to accomplish in and through me with this situation?".

- We can use our struggles to help others going through similar things in their lives. I can think of countless examples where people have become involved with a particular cause or group to help others going through similar difficulties. The reason that I felt compelled to write a book is to share my crazy and my struggles with others in hopes that it will help somehow.

The Scriptures below provide comfort in the face of adversity:

- *"We are hard pressed on every side, but not crushed; perplexed, but not in despair; persecuted, but not abandoned; struck down, but not destroyed" (2 Corinthians 4:8-9).*

- *"Not only so, but we also rejoice in our sufferings, because we know that suffering produces perseverance; perseverance, character; and character, hope" (Romans 5:3 BSB).*

- *"Now the God of all grace, who called you to His eternal glory in Christ Jesus, will personally restore, establish, strengthen, and support you after you have suffered a little" (1 Peter 5:10 HCSB).*

REFLECT

- How have past struggles refined you?

- Where have your struggles defined you?

- What struggles are you experiencing now? How can you use them for good?

66

Pruning My Spiritual Garden

I have a brown thumb. Every new flower or plant that I get dies pretty much immediately. In fact, I think I have killed some of the neighbors' plants simply by walking by. I have never tried to have a garden as I don't think it would fare very well. Even though I haven't taken "Gardening 101" and don't know much, I do know that it's necessary to prune or cut back branches sometimes. Although it appears that it may be destructive at first glance, it is important to cut away dead or overgrown branches to encourage future growth. Similarly, you and I have a spiritual garden—and we need to be "pruned" in different areas of our lives.

In Jesus' final sermon to his disciples, he used a gardening metaphor to describe the importance of growing spiritually and drawing strength from him. *"I am the true vine and my Father is the gardener. He cuts off every branch in me that bears no fruit, while every branch that does bear fruit he prunes so that it will be even more fruitful (John 15:1-2)."*

This means that God must sometimes discipline us to strengthen our character and our faith. Our branches that don't bear fruit are cut off at the trunk because they are of no value and often infect the rest of the tree. Pruning is necessary for us to grow in our walk with God and His Word is the perfect tool for pruning, cleansing, and refreshing us. These Scriptures help us to understand how His Word helps to prune us:

* *"For the Word of God is living and active. Sharper than any double-edged sword, it penetrates even to dividing soul and spirit, joints and marrow; it judges the thoughts and attitudes of the heart"* (Hebrews 4:12).

* *"You are already clean because of the word I have spoken to you"* (John 15:3).

* *"...to make her holy, cleansing her by the washing with water through the word, and to present her to himself as a radiant church, without stain or wrinkle or any other blemish but holy and blameless"* (Ephesians 5:26-27).

Think about your life. Are there things you need to prune or cut off because they are getting in the way of a fruitful relationship with God? There could be things that you need to get rid of, like a bad relationship or something from your past that is dragging you down. Or it could be an idol that is taking your attention away from God.

First Corinthians 10:13 (MSG) is an encouraging Scripture that shows us that God will help us through the pruning process:

> *No test or temptation that comes your way is beyond the course of what others have had to face. All you need to remember is that God will never let you down; he'll never let you be pushed past your limit; he'll always be there to help you come through it.*

Even though it's uncomfortable, the best thing you can do is let God prune you. After the hard part is over, you will see some amazing results! In conclusion, here is a final observation: One of our bushes recently died, and a friend told us that bagworms had eaten it from the inside out. Although I don't think pruning would have helped in this case, maybe it means that we have to keep our insides healthy–full of God and His Word–in order not to die from the inside out. Wow, I'm getting kind of deep.

REFLECT

- What areas of your life do you think need to be "pruned" to further your relationship with God?

67

Spiritual Warrior

"Finally, be strong in the Lord and in his mighty power. Put on the full armor of God, so that you can take your stand against the devil's schemes" (Ephesians 6:10-11).

When things are going well for us, we may not think about it, but we face a spiritual war with an enemy who wants to steal, kill, and destroy. This world is truly a battlefield. We must be wise in resisting Satan's tactics, and nothing can protect us like God's weapons—prayer, faith, hope, love, His Word, and the Holy Spirit.

I've always had a difficult time understanding who Satan is and how he works in our lives. I can't help but picture a red man with horns and a pitchfork as he is often depicted. I know for sure that he is often trying to get in my mind and up in my "bizness." So, I decided to do a little more research on who our enemy is and how he impacts us.

Here are some descriptors of Satan from the Bible:
- He is the Father of lies (John 8:44)
- He leads the whole world astray (Revelation 12:9)
- He is a thief who comes to steal, kill and destroy (John 10:10)
- He prowls around like a roaring lion seeking who he can devour (1 Peter 5:8)
- He disguises himself as an angel of light, attempting to make sin look good and evil enticing (2 Corinthians 11:14)
- He is a tempter who lures with sex, money, power, greed, and lust (Matthew 4:3)
- He lords over what brings death (Matthew 12:23-24)
- He is crafty and manipulative (Genesis 3:1-5)
- He will try everything possible to throw roadblocks in our path and

to stop us from being fruitful (Matthew 16:23, 1 Thessalonians 2:18)

He will attack us:

- In our weakest and most vulnerable moments
- When we don't expect it and let our guard down
- When we think we can handle things and have it all under control
- When we're making a difference for God's purposes

How do we protect ourselves? We need to put on the full armor of God so that we can stand against Satan. The armor of God doesn't sound particularly fashionable or comfortable. But can't be much worse than Spanx and pantyhose. And it's much more beneficial! Let's learn more about this armor of God:

Finally, be strong in the Lord and in his mighty power. Put on the full armor of God, so that you can take your stand against the devil's schemes. For our struggle is not against flesh and blood, but against the rulers, against the authorities, against the powers of this dark world and against the spiritual forces of evil in the heavenly realms. Therefore put on the full armor of God, so that when the day of evil comes, you may be able to stand your ground, and after you have done everything, to stand. Stand firm then, with the belt of truth buckled around your waist, with the breastplate of righteousness in place, and with your feet fitted with the readiness that comes from the gospel of peace. In addition to all this, take up the shield of faith, with which you can extinguish all the flaming arrows of the evil one. Take the helmet of salvation and the sword of the Spirit, which is the Word of God (Ephesians 6:10-18).

As it says above, the components of the armor of God are as follows: the belt of truth, the breastplate of righteousness, the shoes of the gospel, the shield of faith, the helmet of salvation, and the sword of the Spirit.

There are different interpretations, but here's what I got from studying the topic:

- **The belt of truth –** The truths of Scripture as opposed to the lies of Satan.

- **The breastplate of righteousness -** Covers the heart and shields it and the other vital organs. The Bible says, *"Keep your heart with all diligence, for out of it spring the issues of life"* (Proverbs 4:23 NKJV). That is what Christ's righteousness does for you.

- **The shoes of the gospel -** Keeps our feet anchored and standing firm when Satan tries to trip us up.

- **The shield of faith** - Protects us from attacks of the evil one. Roman soldiers carried shields that were covered with heavy animal hide. They would dip their shields into the water before going into battle so that the wet hide would help extinguish fiery darts. Similarly, the shield of faith must be regularly dipped in God's Word.

- **The helmet of salvation** - The knowledge that as believers, we have been rescued from our own wickedness. Our salvation (given to us through our faith in Jesus) says that our sins are forgiven and that we will spend eternity in heaven.

- **The sword of the spirit** - The Word of God is the sword of the Spirit and is the greatest spiritual weapon. When Jesus was tempted in the desert, the Word was always His response to Satan.

In addition to putting on the armor of God every day, here are some things we can do to protect ourselves from the enemy:

- Be alert, have our defenses up, and be ready to protect ourselves – even when it seems that things are going well.

- Submit to God's authority. Resist Satan, and he will flee.

- Know that, in Christ, we are forgiven. We have His mighty power working within us and for us.

- Know that God is for us. He is with us. He fights for us, even when we're not aware. Satan does not have the final say over our lives!

We are spiritual warriors. With God's help, we got this! *"Submit yourselves, then, to God. Resist the devil, and he will flee from you"* (James 4:7).

REFLECT

- What will you do to protect yourself against the enemy?

_____
_____
_____
_____
_____
_____
_____
_____
_____
_____

68
When Things Don't Go as Planned

"A righteous person may have many troubles, but the Lord delivers him from them all; he protects all his bones, not one of them will be broken" (Psalm 34:19-20).

How did you imagine your life? Has it turned out differently than you expected? I feel sure that, for pretty much all of us, life hasn't been exactly as we planned it. Mine certainly hasn't been. But I know that it's not my plan that prevails; it's God's plan. And our plans often do not align. I know His plan is better, but sometimes it doesn't seem like it.

Here are a few of my plans:
- To be rich and famous—kind of kidding here (I never thought I'd be rich and famous. But maybe richER.)
- To be home-free with parenting when the kids went off to college
- To retire by the time I'm 60—probably not happening
- To be well-traveled

Here are some of the things that I DID NOT plan for:
- Life being so hard
- Life going by so fast
- A failed marriage
- A blended family with four kids—never imagined having more than two
- A child who struggled through college with health and physical problems, unhealthy behaviors, emotional problems, drama, etc.
- My stepdaughter getting married to someone she knew for three months and not telling us until after…
- Our kids getting five cats, five dogs, a bearded dragon, and a snake

(Oh, and almost forgot a hedgehog)

- Rainbow hair, piercings (lots of them), and tattoos
- Having the "itises" in my back—arthritis and bursitis

The list goes on, but I'll stop there.

When things don't go as we had planned or expected, we often experience disappointment. Disappointment is defined as the feeling of sadness or displeasure caused by the defeat of one's hopes or expectations.

Whether we like it or not, life should be less about what we desire and more about what God desires for us. As Jesus prayed and asked God to spare Him from suffering on the cross, *"yet not my will, but yours be done"* (Luke 22:42). Jesus wanted his father to take away his suffering but recognized that God's will is what is most important. We should realize that God is working out a plan that is bigger than us and that will be better for us in the end. These Scriptures tell us a little more about His plans for us:

- *"My thoughts are nothing like your thoughts," says the Lord. "And my ways are far beyond anything you could imagine. For just as the heavens are higher than the earth, so my ways are higher than your ways and my thoughts higher than your thoughts"* (Isaiah 55:8-9).

- *"For I know the plans I have for you," says the Lord. "They are plans for good and not for disaster, to give you a future and a hope"* (Jeremiah 29:11 NLT).

When we experience disappointment, we may sometimes want to blame God. But God didn't disappoint us; life's circumstances and other people did. When something disappointing happens in our lives, it's not a time to blame God; it's a time to run to Him!

Here are some positive ways that you can deal with disappointment:

Grieve and then release your disappointment to God

You have experienced a loss, so you will likely need a period where you grieve the situation. Cry, exercise, read, take a trip, or whatever will make you feel better. Face your disappointment and then release it to God. *"The Lord is near to the brokenhearted and saves the crushed in spirit"* (Psalm 34:18 ESV).

Pray

Spend some time talking with God. Tell him how you are feeling and ask him to help you accept your circumstances and move forward with your life.

Assess and adjust your expectations

Assess your situation and then try to readjust your expectations regarding the things you want in life. Place your hope in God and ask Him to help you manage your expectations.

Don't wallow in your disappointment

Instead of wallowing in your disappointment, do something. Help others, take up a new hobby, volunteer. If one dream dies, pick another and keep moving forward.

In her book, *It's Not Supposed to Be This Way*, Lysa TerKeurst says: "Sometimes to get your life back, you have to face the death of what you thought your life would look like." Lysa explains in her book that the human heart was created in the context of perfection in the Garden of Eden. We certainly don't live there now. We live in a broken world where we aren't promised everything we want. God knows what is best for us, and He will deliver us.

REFLECT

- Where have you experienced disappointment in your life?
- Are you currently in a period of disappointment?
- What are some actions you will take to move past it?

_____
_____
_____
_____
_____
_____
_____
_____
_____
_____
_____
_____
_____
_____
_____
_____

69
Disheartening Discouragement

"...but they who wait for the Lord shall renew their strength; they shall mount up with wings like eagles; they shall run and not be weary; they shall walk and not faint" (Isaiah 40:31 ESV).

Are there things happening in your life that are resulting in feelings of discouragement? Do you sometimes feel like you should throw in the towel? I looked up the definition to shed a little more light on the concept of discouragement. It means "to deprive of confidence, hope or spirit; dishearten, daunt."

I felt discouraged as I was finishing this book. Although I was new to writing and certainly had a lot to learn, I poured my blood, sweat, and tears into writing a blog and then a book, and felt a strong conviction that this was something God wanted me to do. I submitted my book to publishers and agents, and the rejections poured in. I then sent out a second wave of proposals and got a yes from a publisher. After more than a year and a half, my book still hadn't been published, so I decided to go another route, and if you are reading this, it finally happened! Discouragement in the short term led to encouragement in the long term with a lot of perseverance!

At work, I am trying to get a Human Resources/organizational development consulting business off the ground. Things are moving a lot slower than I'd like. The pandemic certainly didn't help much. I know that it's in God's timing, but I can't help but feel a little impatient, and yes, discouraged. But I am going to keep at it, with the hopes that it will grow.

We are in good company as it relates to feeling discouraged. I'm pretty sure that most of the people in the Bible felt discouraged at one time or another. Here are a few examples:

- Job felt discouraged because his wife and friends didn't get it. Instead of supporting him, they ended up piling shame and blame on him for his afflictions.

- The disciples felt discouraged when Jesus was crucified as they had put their hope in him to redeem Israel. (Luke 29)

- Peter felt discouraged with himself when he denied Jesus—not once or twice but three times! (John 18)

So, who is behind this sinister force of discouragement? "Could it be–SATAN?!" to quote the Church Lady. For those of you in the younger demographic, this is a character that Dana Carvey played in an old Saturday Night Live skit. If you haven't seen it, check it out on YouTube. (There is actually a chapter about Church Ladies later.) Satan has two primary tools—doubt and discouragement. He wants us to give up and quit!

Here are some strategies to help you overcome feelings of discouragement.

Fill your mind with Scripture.

- *"He heals the brokenhearted and binds up their wounds" (Psalm 147:3).*

- *"Fear not, I am with you; be not dismayed, for I am your God; I will strengthen you, I will help you. I will uphold you with my righteous right hand" (Isaiah 41:10 ESV).*

- *"For I know the plans I have for you, declares the Lord, plans for welfare and not for evil, to give you a future and a hope" (Jeremiah 29:11 ESV).*

- *"...but they who wait for the Lord shall renew their strength; they shall mount up with wings like eagles; they shall run and not be weary; they shall walk and not faint" (Isaiah 40:31 ESV).*

Feel better? These Scriptures have brought me comfort and encouragement.

Train yourself to "see" life out of two lenses at the same time.

In Romans 12:2, the Apostle Paul counsels us to be transformed by the renewing of our minds. I believe that Paul is telling us that our minds need to be trained to think differently than we may have in the past. Part of this training involves seeing both the temporal (life is hard) and the eternal (God has a purpose for this) at the same time.

Paul shares more about the temporal pain when he says he is hard-pressed on every side, perplexed, persecuted, and struck down. Yet, he does not become crushed, filled with despair, abandoned, or destroyed because he firmly fixed the eternal perspective on things above. Paul didn't allow discouragement to win because he knew that God's purposes were being worked out. (2 Corinthians 4:8-9)

Have faith in God and his timing.

We have to remember that God's timeline is not the same as ours. We can't foresee when and how He will work things out, but He has a plan for us that is always better than our plan. *"And let us not grow weary of doing good, for in due season we will reap, if we do not give up"* (Galatians 6:9 ESV).

I am continuing to write, working on another book, and persisting in writing new blog posts. Also, I have ramped up my efforts with the consulting business. This hopefully will set me up for the next step, whatever that may be, in God's timing.

REFLECT

- Is there anything in your life that is making you feel discouraged?
- What will you do to help you overcome these feelings and persevere?

_____
_____
_____
_____
_____
_____
_____
_____
_____
_____
_____
_____
_____
_____
_____
_____
_____
_____
_____
_____
_____
_____

70

Making Insecurity Insignificant

"Since you are precious and honored in my sight, and because I love you, I will give people in exchange for you, nations in exchange for your life" (Isaiah 43:4).

Do you sometimes feel insecure about who you are and where you are going in life? Insecurity is defined as a significant lack of self-confidence, a strong fear of others' disapproval or rejection, or a chronic sense of inferiority. It involves a deep sense of doubt about your worth and place in the world. Insecurity comes in many different shapes and forms. Some people are insecure about their bodies; meanwhile, others are insecure about their work, upbringing, possessions, intelligence, looks, social skills, etc.

Whether we are aware of it or not, our insecurities often seep into our relationships and impact our behavior. Insecurities may stem from past traumas or events you have experienced, often going back to childhood. Maybe you grew up in an unstable or broken home. Or you lost a loved one. Or you were picked on as a child because you were overweight or uncool. Kids can be mean, and bullying and teasing can have a lasting impact. A guy in junior high said that I looked like a Monchhichi doll (Google it). This scarred me, maybe because I kind of did. Then years later, he tried to hit on me—the nerve! But I digress.

To free yourself from insecurity, you have to recognize what is making you insecure. This may take some serious soul searching and prayer. But if you become more aware of your insecurities, it takes away some of their power because you understand when and how they come into play. An example from my own experience relates to my parent's divorce. I went through several bad relationships before realizing that I hadn't worked through some of the feelings and insecurities that resulted from that experience. Once I did, I was able to make better decisions as it related to relationships and ended up with my current husband, who is kind and supportive.

Satan loves it when we question who we are and how we measure up. He wants us to feel insecure about the meaning and purpose of our lives, where we're going, and how we'll get there. Whatever it is that has contributed to your feelings of insecurity, God wants to use for good. He wants to use the situation to refine you. He wants you to grow and mature into a stronger person because of it.

Gideon, a character in the book of Judges, is a great example of someone in the Bible that grappled with overcoming insecurity. While he was harvesting wheat and hiding from the Midianites in a wine press, an angel spoke to him and addressed him as a mighty man of courage. The angel told Gideon that God was sending him to save Israel from the Midianites. Gideon was insecure and didn't feel at all worthy to do this. Look at his response to this request: *"'But Lord,' Gideon replied, 'how can I rescue Israel? My clan is the weakest in the whole tribe of Manasseh, and I am the least in my entire family!'" (Judges 6:15 NLT).*

Gideon was listening to the voice in his head and didn't trust God's plan. We all have these voices from other people—a disapproving parent, a boss, a teacher, or even ourselves. His insecurity caused him to ask God for not just one, but two, miraculous signs to strengthen his faith. This part of Gideon's story shows us that mastering our insecurities doesn't happen in a moment. We will likely have successes and failures. But through it all, God is patient and kind.

To overcome insecurity, we must try to see ourselves the way God sees us and know who we are in Christ. Whenever we feel unloved, unimportant, or insecure, we should remember to whom we belong! (Ephesians 2:19-22) Here are some Scriptures that reinforce this point:

- *"Since you are precious and honored in my sight, and because I love you, I will give people in exchange for you, nations in exchange for your life" (Isaiah 43:4).*

- *"And that is what some of you were. But you were washed, you were sanctified, you were justified in the name of the Lord Jesus Christ and by the Spirit of our God" (1 Corinthians 6:11).*

Did you have a security blanket when you were young? I had a friend that had a blanket that she carried around all the time. Her mother eventually made it into a "blankie coat" so that she could wear it. I like to think of Jesus as my "blankie coat." True security comes when you recognize that God will supply your every need according to His riches in glory in Christ Jesus (Philippians 4:19).

REFLECT

- What are you feeling insecure about in your life?
- How does insecurity manifest itself in your relationships?
- How will you remind yourself of God's love for you and how he sees you when you are feeling insecure?

71
Liberation from Loneliness

Have you ever felt that you were all alone and yearned to feel more connected to others? I'm sure we all have at some point in our lives. The pandemic was certainly a time of loneliness for many. We went through isolations, quarantines and were generally more disconnected from others than ever before.

When I separated from my first husband, the kids went to his house every other weekend. This was the first time that I had been away from them on a regular basis. I felt so very lonely and didn't know what to do with myself. Over time, this got better, and I actually started to somewhat enjoy my alone time. Later in life, the loneliness emerged again when my kids left for college.

There is a difference between loneliness and being alone. You can be in a crowd of people and feel lonely. You can have 500-plus "friends" on social media and feel lonely. You can even be amongst your family and friends and feel lonely.

While it's normal to feel lonely from time to time, ongoing loneliness can have a negative impact on your life. A lonely person may exhibit symptoms like feeling tired, lethargic, and less mentally alert. He or she may experience stomach and digestive problems, and other health issues. A recent Cigna study says that loneliness is at the root of an emerging health crisis. According to one meta-analysis, loneliness increases our odds of dying early by forty-five percent. People who struggle with loneliness may turn to behaviors or substances (often unhealthy) to numb the pain. A few examples include alcohol, drugs, retail therapy, and the media.

David experienced great loneliness and felt forsaken. Instead of blaming God, David drew close to God in his loneliest moments, as is indicated in the Scripture below:

> *Turn to me and be gracious to me, for I am lonely and afflicted. Relieve the troubles of my heart and free me from my anguish. Look on my affliction and my distress and take away all my sins. See how numerous are my enemies and how fierce they hate me! Guard my life and rescue me; do not let me be put to shame, for I take refuge in you. May integrity and uprightness protect me, because my hope, Lord, is in you (Psalm 25:16-21).*

Even Jesus experienced loneliness!

- He was despised and rejected by men (Isaiah 53:3)
- The disciplines forsook Him and fled (Matthew 26:56)
- The crowds shouted, "Crucify him, crucify him! (Luke 23:21)

How can we keep loneliness from getting the best of us?

Read and meditate on God's Word

Have you noticed that this keeps coming up? That's because it's so important! The Bible reminds us that, despite our loneliness, as His beloved children, we are never alone, as is indicated in the Scriptures below:

- *"Even though I walk through the darkest valley, I will fear no evil, for you are with me" (Psalm 23:4).*
- *"Be strong and courageous. Do not be afraid or terrified because of them, for the LORD your God goes with you; he will never leave you nor forsake you" (Deuteronomy 31:16).*
- *"Though my father and mother forsake me, the Lord will receive me" (Psalm 27:10).*
- *"For I am convinced that neither death nor life, neither angels nor demons, neither the present nor the future, nor any powers, neither height nor depth, nor anything else in all creation, will be able to separate us from the love of God that is in Christ Jesus our Lord" (Romans 8:38-29).*

Reach out to others.

"For none of us lives for ourselves alone, and none of us dies for ourselves alone" (Romans 14:7). Some of us may wait for God to send people our way to counteract our loneliness. While He may lead others to befriend us, we may need to take some initiative to reach out to others. Work to build a network of other Christians to help strengthen and encourage you.

Reframe your thinking about being alone.

"But Jesus often withdrew to lonely places and prayed" (Luke 5:16). Loneliness isn't necessarily a bad thing. Jesus set the example for us by withdrawing to lonely places to spend time with His Father. There are times in our lives when we need to pull away from people to reconnect and hear from God.

Serve others.

It's hard to be lonely when we are serving others. Get involved in your community by volunteering at your church or with non-profit organizations. Find ways to humbly love and serve the people you meet.

REFLECT

- Reflect on and write down some times in your life when you experienced loneliness.

- If you are in a period of loneliness in your life now, how can you use this to enhance your relationship with the Lord?

_____
_____
_____
_____
_____
_____
_____
_____
_____
_____
_____
_____
_____
_____
_____
_____
_____
_____
_____
_____
_____
_____
_____
_____

72

Turning a Setback into a Comeback!

"And the God of all grace, who called you to his eternal glory in Christ, after you have suffered a little while, will himself restore you and make you strong, firm and steadfast" (1 Peter 5:10).

Have you ever encountered a setback where something unexpected messed up your plans and resulted in feelings of discouragement and disappointment? Maybe your setback involved a failed relationship, a health issue, a financial problem, or a curveball in your career or education. Setbacks cause delays, inconvenience and cause you to question the direction your life is headed. This doesn't mean that setbacks are failures. Setbacks don't have to define your future.

By the time you get to fifty-something, you have likely experienced multiple setbacks in your life. And survived! I know I have, and some of my setbacks truly resulted in something even better that God had for me. My daughter recently experienced a major setback in her chosen career path, which resulted in another year of school. She felt discouraged and beaten down, but I know God has a greater plan for her in the end.

Many great people faced setbacks in their lives. Michael Jordan was cut from his high school basketball team. Thomas Edison failed multiple times in inventing the light bulb. Walt Disney was fired from a job for not being creative enough. These individuals obviously got back up and kept going, achieving great success and inspiring us all.

The Bible is full of stories where men and women experienced serious setbacks. Here are a few:

- Joseph's brothers sold him into slavery. He ended up in prison but eventually became the Pharaoh's right-hand man over all of Egypt.

- Esther was sentenced to marry a king who had his previous wife killed. Just weeks after getting married, her new husband unwittingly signed a decree that all of Ether's people should be eliminated. She went before the king and made an appeal for her people and was ultimately successful.

- Paul was put in prison and experienced many unexpected delays in his efforts to spread the gospel. In Philippians 4:11-12 (ESV), he wrote,

    > ...for I have learned in whatever situation I am to be content. I know how to be brought low, and I know how to abound. In any and every circumstance, I have learned the secret of facing plenty and hunger, abundance, and need.

What did these individuals have in common? They trusted in God and sought His help in difficult times. When things didn't go as desired, they maintained a positive attitude because they knew God would make all things work out according to His purpose. If you are feeling discouraged over an apparent setback, remember these examples.

Here are five things to do after suffering a setback:

1. **Assess your situation.** Think about what you can learn from the situation. How did you get there? What could you have done differently? What are your options now?

2. **Take a break.** You may need to rest and recuperate after the setback. This isn't the same thing as giving up. Fatigue may have even contributed to the setback, so take some time to rest.

3. **Ask for help.** First, ask God for His guidance and assistance. You may also want to ask someone else you trust for advice on your next steps.

4. **Trust God.** Trust that your Creator will carry you through the setback or trial. Refamiliarize yourself with how great He is. This can help calm you down and put things into perspective.

5. **Don't give up.** Many people give up when things don't go their way. If you feel that you should proceed with your original plans, then do so. Or, if you think you may need to reassess your path and change course, do that. But don't throw in the towel!

Finally, stop focusing on the past and focus on Him.

Brothers, I do not consider that I have made it my own. But one thing I do: forgetting what lies behind and straining forward to what lies ahead, I press on toward the goal for the prize of the upward call of God in Christ Jesus. Let those of us who are mature think this way, and if in anything you think otherwise, God will reveal that also to you (Philippians 3:13-15 ESV).

In conclusion, remember, it's just a setback. It's not your future. God may be orchestrating something unexpectedly good in your life, despite the reversal of your plans. Turn your setback into a comeback!

REFLECT

- Have you ever experienced a setback in your life? If so, how did you deal with it?
- How will you use these tips to put current or future setbacks in perspective?

73

GRIEF- Grace Results in Enduring Hope for Us

I recently lost my mother unexpectedly. It has been quite difficult as we were very close. I know that, with God, I will get through it, but it sure is hard. Unfortunately, the terrible pain of losing a loved one is something almost everyone experiences. No matter how imminent the death, nothing prepares us for the emotional rollercoaster that we will encounter. We won't see our loved one's face again in this life. We won't enjoy their company. We won't be able to tell them how much we love them.

Although there are generally stages of grief, each person sets his or her own pace. There will be ups and downs, moments of relief followed by moments of anguish. C.S. Lewis said, "Grief turns out to be not a state but a process. Grief is like a winding road where any bend may reveal a totally new landscape." In Matthew 5:4, Jesus says, *"blessed are those who mourn, for they will be comforted..."* Jesus is implying that God cares deeply for everyone and hears all who call out to him. He will be with us during our darkest moments of sorrow.

I created the acronym below to illustrate the comfort and hope that God brings amid the grief process:

- **G** Grace
- **R** Results
- **I** In
- **E** Enduring hope
- **F** For Us

We can have consolation in the thought that God has showered His grace on our loved one, and he/she is now in a peaceful place with no more pain or sorrow. Through His loving grace, He will help us to overcome our sorrow. Lately, as I have been feeling overwhelmed by grief, I have been praying Psalm 119:28: *"My soul is weary with sorrow; strengthen me according to your word."*

John 16:33 (ESV) says, *"In the world you will have tribulation. But take heart; I have overcome the world."* In this passage, Jesus says we will endure suffering, yet our hope is not in what we experience on earth. Our enduring hope can be found in Jesus Christ alone and the undeserved grace and love He gives to us.

<u>REFLECT</u>

- If you are currently experiencing grief, I hope you find comfort in this lesson.

SECTION 6:

Everything Else

Leslie Speas

74

Get Out of Jail Free Card

"So now there is no condemnation for those who belong to Christ Jesus. And because you belong to him, the power of the life-giving Spirit has freed you from the power of sin that leads to death" (Romans 8:1-2 NLT).

A second chance is a declaration that you are not holding a person's past against him/her but expect to see positive changes in his/her life. I believe in second chances. We all have needed a second chance at some point in our lives. The fact is, we all fail. We all do things we are ashamed of. We all say things we regret. We all hurt people we care about. Even Paul was no stranger to failure as he says, *"I do not understand the things I do. I do not do what I want to do, and I do the things I hate"* (Romans 7:15 NCV).

During my career, I have been involved in helping many people receive a second chance for employment. I have worked for several organizations where we have hired folks with criminal records and even some who were in jail for an extended time. I have seen some people rise to the occasion, overcome their challenges, and lead a successful, productive life. I have seen others that have fallen back into old patterns. However, I genuinely believe that we all deserve a second—and maybe even a third, fourth, and fifth chance. God is patient in giving us second chances—and not just one, but continual chances. Micah 7:18 says, *"Who is a God like you, who pardons sin and forgives the transgression of the remnant of his inheritance? You do not stay angry forever but delight to show mercy."*

I remember a man who had been in prison for larceny that we hired at a former employer soon after he was released. He had participated in the prison ministry program, and we received a favorable reference from the Chaplain. He rode his bike across town every day to come to work and showed great promise. He was willing to pitch in and do whatever was needed. One day, he stopped reporting to work, and we later saw in the paper that he had been arrested for robbing a bank. He wrote me a letter from prison and said that he tried to turn his life around, but his demons were too much for him to handle. This was very disappointing. However, I have been inspired by others that have risen to the occasion and become good employees, even moving into leadership roles. We have all sinned and fallen short of the glory of God. But He continues to support us and love us. I believe we should do the same for others.

Remember Rahab? Like many women back in her day, she chose the world's oldest profession to earn a living (prostitution, in case you didn't know). Through a series of events, Rahab bargained for her life with two Israelite spies and hid them in her home. Consequently, she and her family survived the destruction of her country. She then went on to marry one of the men and became a grandmother in the lineage of Jesus Christ (many times removed but still a grandmother). Talk about a comeback!

Here are some additional examples of folks from the Bible who needed (and received) a second chance:

- Noah was found drunk by his sons
- Abraham trafficked his wife
- David hired someone for murder and committed adultery
- Zacchaeus overtaxed people due to personal greed
- Peter denied Christ three times

God gave them a second chance—despite their immoral and illegal actions. They repented and went on to serve as His faithful servants.

Jesus came to earth and died to pay the penalty of our failures and, if we receive him, his record becomes our record. And his record couldn't be any better! He has given us all second chances—and probably many more than that. Shouldn't we do the same for others? By walking alongside those who need a second chance, we can help bring God's healing into their lives.

> *"But this I call to mind, and therefore I have hope: The steadfast love of the Lord never ceases; his mercies never come to an end; they are new every morning; great is your faithfulness"* (Lamentations 3:21-23 ESV).

REFLECT

- When have you needed a second chance in your life?
- How can you help someone who needs a second chance?

_____
_____
_____
_____

Fearless Faith

"Don't be afraid; just believe" (Mark 5:36).

I know some people who seem to have unshakeable faith in God—no matter what struggles, trials or disappointments come their way. Unfortunately, I am often not one of those people. My faith often wavers, especially when I'm undergoing difficulties. Instead of trusting in God, I sometimes plan, doubt, worry, fret, and try to control. Currently, I have several situations in my life that I am fervently praying about. I'm not seeing progress on my timeline, so I keep trying to insert myself to facilitate forward movement. At least now that I'm a little more mature in my faith, I'm conscious when I'm doing this and able to redirect myself towards faith.

What is faith? Hebrews 11:1 provides a definition, *"Now faith is confidence in what we hope for and assurance about what we do not see."* Faith is the result of believing the good news that Jesus died for our sins and that we can be saved by faith. Faith causes us to act on what we haven't experienced yet, trust promises in the Bible that haven't yet been fulfilled, and trust God while we wait for our situations to change.

Hebrews is like the faith hall of fame. Honorable mentions in Hebrews 11 include Abel, Enoch, Noah, Abraham, and more. In my opinion, one of the most amazing acts of faith in the Bible is Abraham's willingness to give up his long-awaited son when God asked him to.

Here are a few of the many benefits of faith:
- Faith produces joy and peace (Romans 15:13)
- Faith expresses itself through love for others (Galatians 5:6)
- Faith results in obedience (Hebrews 11:8)
- Faith extinguishes all of the flaming arrows of the evil one (Ephesians 6:16)
- Faith conquers the sinful pull of the world (1 John 5:4)
- Faith helps us to be men (and women) of courage (1 Corinthians 16:13)

- Faith makes us bold with strength in our soul (Psalm 138)

I don't know how people get through the difficult seasons in life if they don't have faith. I don't want to imagine a life where there isn't a God to place my faith in.

If you struggle with your faith, here are some things that you can do:

Ask

In Mark 9:14-29 (ESV), when a man with a demon-possessed son cried to Jesus, *"I believe; help my unbelief."* Jesus responded by strengthening the man's faith. Likewise, we can ask God to strengthen our faith.

Listen

Romans 10:17 (ESV) says, *"So faith comes from hearing, and hearing through the word of Christ."* The answer to weak faith is returning to the source of our faith and immersing ourselves in His Word.

Choose

Ultimately, I believe that faith is a choice. It means seizing God's promises despite how weak and downcast we may be. The more we choose to believe, the easier it becomes. When my faith starts to waver, I ask myself what the alternative is. When I think about that, it quickly redirects me to put my faith in God. Faith can do a lot of things in your life if you let it. It will grow you and allow you to do things you never thought yourself capable of.

> *"Whoever believes in me, as Scripture has said, rivers of living water will flow from within them"* (John 7:38).

REFLECT

- Does your faith waver at times? If so, in what situations?
- What will you do to strengthen your faith?

_____
_____
_____
_____
_____
_____
_____

76

Heavenly Hope

"As for me, I will always have hope; I will praise you more and more" (Psalm 71:14).

What are some of the things that you hope for in your life? Here are some of mine:

- I hope that I will make a difference in the lives of others.
- I hope for good health for my family and myself.
- I hope that God answers my prayers.
- I hope to have financial security.
- I hope to be able to retire one day.
- I hope that I will go to heaven.
- I hope I win the lottery—okay, that one isn't very biblical or realistic.

Let's explore the definition of hope. Hope is "a feeling of expectation and desire for a certain thing to happen." We talked about faith. So, what's the difference between faith and hope? Faith says it is so now, and hope says it could happen in the future. Hope is basically the soil in which we exercise our faith.

Where is your hope? Many of us place our hope in other people, our careers, material possessions, the government, the economy, etc. Placing our hope in anything but God is like expecting a tree to grow and flourish in the barren desert. We will be disappointed every time, and our deepest needs will never be satisfied. The Lord is the only one that can truly do that.

Here are some of the advantages of placing our hope in God:

- **Hope renews our strength:** *"...but those who hope in the Lord will renew their strength. They will soar on wings like eagles; they will run and not grow weary, they will walk and not be faint"* (Isaiah 40:31).

- **Hope brings us security:** *"You will be secure, because there is hope;*

you will look about you and take your rest in safety" (Job 11:18).

- **Hope brings joy:** *"Be joyful in hope" (Romans 12:12).*

- **Hope brings love:** *"And hope does not put us to shame, because God's love has been poured out into our hearts through the Holy Spirit, who has been given to us" (Romans 5:5).*

I love these lyrics from the song, "Living Hope" by Phil Wickham:

> Hallelujah, praise the One who set me free
> Hallelujah, death has lost its grip on me
> You have broken every chain
> There's salvation in Your name
> Jesus Christ, my living hope

Our world is uncertain and is filled with violence, confusion, fear, and hopelessness. I choose to experience the world through the lens of hope in the living God. Will you?

REFLECT

- What are you currently hoping for?

- How can you place all of your hope in God?

77

Joy to the World

"Rejoice always; pray continually; give thanks in all circumstances, for this is God's will for you in Christ Jesus" (1 Thessalonians 5:16-18).

"Joy to the World" by Three Dog Night is one of my favorite songs. I never could figure out why Jeremiah was a bullfrog who had fine wine. Unfortunately, you won't find out the answer to that here.

Would you like to experience joy on a daily basis? This world is void of joy and full of negative emotions such as fear, worry, and disappointment. I don't feel joyful much of the time, which inspired me to research this topic and learn more about joy. Honestly, my life is pretty great compared to much of the world's population. I have a roof over my head, food to eat, heat/air condition, a loving family, good health, and I'm not living in a war zone. I should feel joyful, right?

You often hear joy and happiness being used interchangeably, but they aren't the same. Happiness is a glad feeling or emotion which depends on something good happening. It is circumstantial and increases and decreases depending on what's going on in our lives. Joy is rooted in an intimate relationship with God. As we grow closer to Him, we also grow in joy.

I love this quote from S.D. Gordon that further helps to define joy and further differentiates it from happiness:

> Joy is distinctly a Christian word and a Christian thing. It is the reverse of happiness. Happiness is the result of what happens of an agreeable sort. Joy has its springs deep down inside. And that spring never runs dry, no matter what happens. Only Jesus gives that joy. He had joy, singing its music within, even under the shadow of the cross.

In our world, we're taught to value possessions, power, and position. But true joy is not found in those things. Here are some Scriptures that demonstrate how we can find joy:

- *"I am the vine; you are the branches. If you remain in me and I in you, you will bear much fruit; apart from me you can do nothing"* (John 15:5).

- *"…then make my joy complete by being like-minded, having the same love, united in spirit and purpose"* (Philippians 2:2 BSB).

A person can experience joy even when they are undergoing difficult circumstances. For example, we can have joy when someone close to us dies, even though we are sad and grieving. If that person was a Christian, we know that they are at peace and with God. We can find joy in any circumstance in our relationship with God. James 1:2 tells us to *"Consider it pure joy, my brothers and sisters, whenever you face trials of many kinds."*

Paul speaks about joy and about the Christian's duty to rejoice over and over again. For example, he writes, *"Rejoice in the Lord always"* (Philippians 4:4). He doesn't say "rejoice sometimes when things are good." He tells us to rejoice always and even adds, *"Again I will say, Rejoice."*

Joy is also grounded in the idea that something is good for someone else. We experience joy when we are contributing to someone else's well-being. The world is full of lonely, hurting people. Reach out to someone else that could use your help.

To grow in joy, we must resist focusing on ourselves and focus on loving others and especially on loving God. If we truly believe what God says to us in the Bible, then we have plenty to rejoice about.

In conclusion, joy is meant to be part of the Christian life. It is a fruit of the Holy Spirit and a gift from God. We can receive this gift when we focus on who God is, spend time with Him through prayer, and rely on the community of believers He has provided.

REFLECT

- Do you regularly have feelings of joy in your life?
- What will you do to lead a more joyful life?

_____
_____
_____
_____
_____
_____
_____
_____
_____
_____

78

Laughter Is the Best Medicine

I love to laugh. Watching Jimmy Fallon is one of my favorite things, as I think he is hilarious. And for anyone who cares, he is also my celebrity crush. I'm hoping to be a guest on his show when this book is published (kidding). I'm also pretty good at laughing at myself, as you can probably tell from this book. There is certainly a lot of material.

I have often wondered if God has a sense of humor. I think he does. He created us, so how can we think things are funny unless the whole idea came from Him in the first place? He also created some pretty funny creatures like manatees and warthogs. And let's face it, our bodily functions are rather humorous. And there are so many funny absurdities in life in general.

Some of the things that are in the Bible are pretty humorous as well. Remember when God used a donkey to speak to Balaam? (Numbers 22) The Book of Proverbs can be pretty funny at times. One example is Proverbs 11:22, which says, *"Like a gold ring in a pig's snout is a beautiful woman who shows no discretion."*

So, what does the Bible say about laughter? *"He will yet fill your mouth with laughter and your lips with shouts of joy"* (Job 8:21). In this verse, Job's friend is reminding him that God is with us and will restore our joy in the end. Ecclesiastes 3:4 says there is a *"time to weep and a time to laugh, a time to mourn and a time to dance."* So, laugh when it's time to laugh; it feels good!

When Sarah overheard God telling Abraham that she would have a child, she laughed. I probably would have too. Sarah was very advanced in age. Her laugh was due to disbelief, but when her son was born, she named him Isaac, which means "he laughs."

Proverbs 17:22 says, *"A cheerful heart is good medicine, but a crushed spirit dries up the bones."* So the saying "Laughter is the best medicine" goes back to ancient times. And laughter actually does have health benefits. It lightens your load mentally and has many physical health benefits. Studies have shown that it boosts the immune system and triggers the release of pleasure-inducing neurochemicals in the brain.

The Bible reminds us that it is good not to take life too seriously. The woman in Proverbs 31 *"is clothed with strength and dignity, and she laughs without fear of the future" (verse 25).*

Here are some ways to bring more humor and laughter into your life:

- **Smile-** Smiling is the beginning of laughter. So do it more!

- **Count your blessings-** Make a list of all of your blessings. The simple act of considering the good things in your life will distance you from negative thoughts, which are a barrier to laughter.

- **Spend time with people who make you laugh-** These are people who laugh easily, both at themselves and at life's absurdities, and who can routinely make you laugh.

- **Laugh at yourself-** Share your embarrassing and amusing moments. Get over yourself, and don't take yourself so seriously.

- **Watch movies, TV shows, or read things that make you laugh-** I mentioned Jimmy Fallon as one of my favs. Movies that make me laugh include There's Something About Mary, Meet the Fockers, and Talladega Nights. My favorite funny TV shows include Friends and The Office.

- **Emulate children-** They are the experts on taking life lightly and laughing!

If you suspect you might be suffering from a lack of cheer, use some of the suggestions above to bring more laughter into your life!

> *"Then our mouth was filled with laughter, and our tongue with shouts of joy; then they said among the nations, 'The Lord has done great things for them'" (Psalm 126:2 ESV).*

REFLECT

- How will you use some of this information to bring more laughter into your life?

_____
_____
_____
_____
_____
_____
_____

He Is with Me Always

"You have searched me, Lord, and you know me. You know when I sit and when I rise; you perceive my thoughts from afar. You discern my going out and my lying down; you are familiar with all my ways" (Psalm 139:1-3).

It is amazing to think that God is always with us through his Holy Spirit. In my quiet time, I was reading a devotional, *Unblinded Faith: Gaining Spiritual Sight Through Believing God's Word*, by Elisa Pulliam. She shared part of the verse above and asked the question, "How would it change your relationship with God to settle into the truth that He is always watching over you, whatever you do and wherever you go?" I reflected on this question and decided to take Jesus with me as a passenger for a few days—wherever I went and whatever I did. As if He wasn't already there! But I tried to be more conscious of His presence.

Buckle up, Lord, it's going to be a wild ride, or maybe I should say mild (rather boring) ride. During this time, I tried to stay mindful of Him throughout the day and even had little discussions with him—silently so that my coworkers didn't think I was crazier than they already do. He went to work with me. When picturing him in a meeting, I thought a little more about my behavior (although I don't usually get out of hand). I should have tried this at my last employer, where the meetings generally involved drama and tension.

He also exercised with me, walked the dogs, and even got to experience some hot flashes. We watched a little Netflix. I wasn't sure the show was appropriate, so we switched to reading instead. The experience made me more conscious of Him as I went through my day and gave me a sense of peace and comfort. I think I will consciously "take Him with me" a little more often.

The Scriptures below remind us that he is ever-present in our lives:
- *"...the Lord will watch over your coming and going both now and forevermore" (Psalm 121:8).*
- *"Have I not commanded you? Be strong and courageous. Do not be frightened, and do not be dismayed, for the Lord your God is with you wherever you go" (Joshua 1:9 ESV).*

- *"...and teaching them to observe all that I have commanded you. And surely, I am with you always, to the very end of the age"* (Matthew 28:20 BSB).

When you are feeling bad about yourself or need some encouragement, remember that God's spirit is within you.

REFLECT

- How would it impact your relationship with God if you were conscious of Him watching over you throughout the day? How might it change your behavior?

_____
_____
_____
_____
_____
_____
_____
_____
_____
_____
_____
_____
_____
_____
_____
_____
_____
_____
_____
_____
_____
_____

80

How Do You Want to Be Remembered?

I don't know about you but, as I get older, time seems to fly by. I love the song "Dust in the Wind" by Kansas. It's a little depressing but true. We only have a short time on this earth, and we truly are dust in the wind in the greater scheme of things.

Here are some Scriptures that remind us of the brevity of life:
- "What is your life? You are a mist that appears for a little while and then vanishes" (James 5:14).
- "He remembered that they were but flesh, a wind that passes and comes not again" (Psalm 78:39 ESV).

As we get older, the days of our youth become a distant memory. Our college years fade into the distance. Our children grow up and have babies of their own. We certainly become more in touch with our mortality and wonder what impact we are having on the world. Now that I have depressed everyone, let's talk a little about legacy. If you left this life today, how would others remember you? What would be your legacy?

In 2 Timothy 4:7-8, Paul ponders the end of his life in a letter to his friend, Timothy. He made three simple statements about his legacy as follows:
- He had fought the good fight—putting on the armor of God and fighting the good fight every day
- He had finished the race—running his race in a focused and dedicated way; striving not for a temporary crown, but an eternal one
- He kept the faith—was always faithful, and fulfilled his divine appointment in this world

Sounds like a pretty good legacy to me! How many of us will be able to say the same?

At the end of life, I don't think most people are concerned about the possessions they have accumulated, the places they have traveled, their education, or the career success they have experienced. I believe they are more concerned about their relationships with God and the people they love. I also believe that most people hope that they somehow made a positive impact on the world.

I hope that I will be able to share Paul's legacy at the end of my life. I hope to have used my spiritual gifts and talents for good and lived out God's purpose for me. Also, I hope that I will have been a blessing in the lives of others and that my life somehow pointed others closer to Christ. I have some work to do because sometimes I might be more of a "lesson" than a "blessing."

> *"Forgetting what is behind and straining toward what is ahead, I press on toward the goal to win the prize for which God has called me heavenward in Christ Jesus"* (Hebrews 3:13-14).

REFLECT

- If you left this world today, how do you think you would be remembered?
- How would you like to be remembered?

81

Christians Can Have Fun Too!

When I was younger, I wasn't sure that I wanted to be a Christian because I thought Christians couldn't really have fun. I had a friend when I was growing up whose family was very religious. She wasn't allowed to do certain things or see PG movies, and she had to go to church several times a week. As a teenager, she didn't go to parties. Full disclosure, I did my share of partying in high school and college. At the time, I thought that her life as a Christian was pretty lame. I changed my tune a bit when my kids reached their teenage years!

Unfortunately, I wasn't brought up being very involved in church and wasn't that knowledgeable about Christianity. I also didn't have the benefit of a youth group or college ministry to help me learn, build a relationship with God, and stay grounded. I established my relationship with Jesus later in life and realized that Christians can most certainly have fun.

Let's explore the concept of "fun" a little more. The American Heritage Dictionary defines fun as "a source of enjoyment, amusement, or pleasure." What is considered "fun" is obviously different for different people. My sister-in-law thinks hiking the Appalachian Trail is fun, while I think it would be pretty awful. I'm fine with some day hiking as long as there is a nice hotel (preferably four-star) to stay in at night. And there can be no snakes, mice, or anything gross. My idea of fun might include boutique shopping which probably is not on my sister-in-law's top ten list of fun activities.

I think that God wants us to have fun and celebrate so we can see the beauty and meaning in the life that He has created for us. There are many celebrations cited in the Bible, with a few examples below:

- "Wearing a linen ephod, David, was dancing before the Lord with all his might, while he and all Israel were bringing up the ark of the Lord with shouts and the sound of trumpets" (2 Samuel 6:14-15).

- "On the third day, a wedding took place at Cana in Galilee. Jesus' mother was there, and Jesus and his disciples had also been invited to the wedding. When the wine was gone, Jesus' mother said to him, 'They have no more wine,' 'Dear woman, why do you involve me?' Jesus replied. 'My time has not yet come.' His mother said

> to the servants, 'Do whatever he tells you.' Nearby stood six stone water jars, the kind used by the Jews for ceremonial washing, each holding from twenty to thirty gallons. Jesus said to the servants. 'Fill the jars with water,' so they filled them to the brim. Then he told them, 'Now draw some out and take it to the master of the banquet.' They did so, and the master tasted the water that had been turned into wine" (John 2:1-9).

God has placed us on earth with many activities to participate in and lots of other people to have fun with. He created in us the ability to be amused and to laugh. He has allowed us to discover music, pizza, chocolate, cake, games, and roller coasters. Those are indicators that He wants us to enjoy our lives.

Christians may find fun in some things that non-Christians do not. Examples may include worshipping and serving others. Also, I believe that Christians may feel free to have more fun. They can "let go and let God" when it comes to dealing with difficulties in their lives and know that their sins have been forgiven on the cross. This allows them to live more in the present and enjoy the little things with their burdens lifted.

Some activities may seem fun at the time but can have long-term physical and spiritual consequences. If the "fun" activity involves sin or is self-involved or indulgent, it will take away from your faith. Sin doesn't need to be part of something to make it fun. There is plenty of fun to be had outside of sin!

These Scriptures shed a little more light on how sin impacts fun:
- *"The light of the righteous shines brightly, but the lamp of the wicked is snuffed out"* (Proverbs 13:9).
- *"For you have spent enough time in the past doing what pagans choose to do—living in debauchery, lust, drunkenness, orgies, carousing and detestable idolatry"* (1 Peter 4:3).

Full disclosure again, I love me some wine. And I think it's okay as long as I don't regularly overindulge or let it lead me into sinful activities. Many people in our world today seem to seek fun over God, which is problematic. Matthew 6:33 says, *"But first seek his kingdom and his righteousness, and all these things will be given to you as well."* If we don't take this verse seriously, it would be easy for us to place fun and many other things before God.

I will end this chapter by sharing a quote that I liked a lot. I don't know about you, but I want to be part of the kingdom of divine laughter!

> Laughter is a divine gift to the human who is humble. A proud man cannot laugh because he must watch his dignity; he cannot give himself over to the rocking and rolling of his belly. But a poor and

happy man laughs heartily because he gives no serious attention to his ego…

Only the truly humble belong to this kingdom of divine laughter… Humor and humility should keep good company. Self-deprecating humor can be a healthy reminder that we are not the center of the universe, that humility is our proper posture before our fellow humans as well as before almighty God (*Surprised by Laughter: The Comic World of C.S. Lewis* by Terry Lindvall).

REFLECT

- Think about things you do that you think are fun (if any involve sin, re-evaluate your idea of fun and incorporate some other activities).

82
What Should I Do in My Quiet Time?

"But whoever looks intently into the perfect law that gives freedom, and continues in it—not forgetting what they have heard, but doing it—they will be blessed in what they do" (James 1:25).

Have you considered having daily quiet time but aren't sure what to do? I know I have struggled. I have tried reading from the Bible using a "read the Bible in a year" format. I got stuck in Leviticus. I have tried reading devotions, but I tend to finish quickly, so I end up doing a few at one sitting. I think you are supposed to read the devotions and reflect and meditate on them, but I am a skimmer. I have tried sitting in silence, but my mind does its usual "all over the place" exercise. All this to say, I have not perfected the practice, but I keep trying! Even though what I do certainly isn't perfect, it has certainly changed my life for the better!

In John 15:1-4, Jesus said,
I am the true vine, and my Father is the gardener. He cuts off every branch in me that bears no fruit, while every branch that does bear fruit he prunes so that it will be even more fruitful. You are already clean because of the word I have spoken to you. Remain in me, as I also remain in you. No branch can bear fruit by itself; it must remain in the vine. Neither can you bear fruit unless you remain in me.

This tells us that, through the discipline of maintaining that connection to Jesus (the vine), we are personally transformed and become fruitful.

Although I certainly have not perfected this practice, here are some tips for establishing and keeping a meaningful quiet time each day:

Schedule time

Decide on the amount of time that you will dedicate and put it on your schedule. Morning is ideal because it sets the tone for the day, but any time you can fit it in is good. Psalm 5:3 says, *"In the morning, Lord, you hear my voice; in the morning I lay my requests before you and wait expectantly."*

Whatever time you choose, start with 10 to 15 minutes and practice it regularly. As you accomplish this, it will be easier to increase the time you spend.

Pick a place

Pick a place where you'll have your quiet time each day. Think about where you will be comfortable and can focus with as little distraction as possible.

Decide on the format

Think about how you will structure your quiet time. What feels most important to you? Sitting quietly with God, praying, reading the Bible, doing a devotion, listening to worship music, journaling, doing a Bible Study, or some combination. You can change the format over time and do combinations of each of these things. The goal is not to be mechanical but rather to provide some structure, which will lead to building a closer relationship with the Lord. Don't worry as much about what activities you are doing at this point; just do something.

Do it with discipline

Commit to having quiet time consistently for at least thirty days. Do it… whether you "feel" like it or not. If you miss the exact time, make it up later in the day. Just like with any new habit, you'll have to establish discipline, or obstacles will surely get in the way. I can assure you that Satan will try to do things to get in the way of your quiet time!

As usual, Jesus sets the example for us. He took time to connect with the Father regularly, as the following Scriptures tell us:

- *"Then Jesus went with his disciples to a place called Gethsemane, and he said to them, 'Sit here while I go over there and pray'"* (Matthew 26:36).

- *"Very early in the morning, while it was still dark, Jesus got up, left the house and went off to a solitary place, where he prayed"* (Mark 1:35).

- *"But Jesus often withdrew to lonely places and prayed"* (Luke 5:16).

When we set aside time to truly connect with God, our relationship with Him will grow, leading to spiritual transformation in our lives.

REFLECT

- How will you start to practice quiet time each day?

- If you are already practicing, how might you enhance your time with God?

83

Divine Discernment

"Whether you turn to the right or to the left, your ears will hear a voice behind you, saying, 'This is the way; walk in it.'" (Isaiah 30:21).

The GPS is a great invention. I don't know how I ever got anywhere before they were a thing. I am directionally challenged and can't read a map. Funny story, my first GPS was a TomTom. Remember those? I was using it for the first time driving to Atlanta. As somewhat of a joke, my husband set it to "moo" like a cow anytime I went over the speed limit. It scared me to death at first, and being somewhat technically challenged, I did not know how to cut it off.

Have you ever wished that you had a GPS to tell you where to turn at each juncture when it comes to making decisions? Unfortunately, it doesn't usually work that way. Someone close to me is at a crossroads in her life and soon will have to make a big decision related to her chosen career. I'm hoping this chapter will help her and others make decisions in line with God's will.

I don't necessarily think we need to seek God's guidance on things like whether we should have Cheerios or Special K for breakfast or what outfit we should wear to an event. But we face some big decisions in life where we unquestionably need God's support. This could include decisions related to marriage, kids, jobs, relocation, and more.

Here are some things that you can do to try to discern God's will in your decision-making process:

Consult God's Word

The Bible is the guide for our lives. You don't have to take a shot in the darkness of decision-making.

"Your word is a lamp for my feet, a light on my path" (Psalm 119:105).

When it comes to making decisions, much of what we need to know is quite obvious in Scripture. If your decision is about cheating on your spouse, you don't have to dig very far to find the answer. But if it's something less clear, you may need to do some additional investigation to get help with your answer.

Pray

We communicate with God through prayer. Pray about the decision and ask for his guidance and direction in the process. Be careful not to confuse God's voice with your feelings and desires.

Listen to your inner conviction

Inner conviction from the Holy Spirit will always be in line with God's will for us and is therefore critical for making the right decisions. How do we know what this is? I don't know for sure, but I know that I often feel a nudge in one direction or another and have a feeling of peace when I think about making that choice. I believe that is coming from the Holy Spirit.

Consider your circumstances

God can open and close doors. He may use events in your life to point you in a certain direction. For example, maybe you are thinking of moving but aren't sure what to do. If your house catches on fire, this would be a huge hint that moving would be a good decision.

> "These are the words of him who is holy and true, who holds the key of David. What he opens no one can shut, and what he shuts no one can open" (Revelation 3:7).

Seek the counsel of Christian friends

Approach some trusted friends and ask for their insights and guidance. You might share the options, the details of the situation, and what you feel God is saying to you. Then listen and consider how their counsel can help inform your decision.

Follow peace

One way that we can be certain we are hearing from God is to follow peace. He may lead us to make sudden changes, but He will always give us His peace in the midst of it.

> "Let the peace of Christ rule in your hearts…" (Colossians 3:15).

James 3:15-17 gives us the characteristics of godly wisdom.
Such 'wisdom' does not come down from heaven but is earthly, unspiritual, demonic. For where you have envy and selfish ambition, there you find disorder and every evil practice. But the wisdom that comes from heaven is first of all pure; then peace-loving, considerate, submissive, full of mercy and good fruit, impartial and sincere.
Ask yourself whether your choice meets these qualifications. This can help you

discern whether you are on the right path.

REFLECT

- What is your current process when it comes to making a big decision?

- What will you do going forward to make sure that your decisions are in line with His will?

84

Down with the Drama!

"Blessed are the peacemakers, for they will be called sons of God" (Matthew 5:9 BSB).

Are you tired of dealing with drama in your life? Do you know anyone that you would classify as a drama queen or king? Do you sometimes create drama yourself?

As I have gotten older, I have less tolerance for drama. I just want to be around peaceful people, doing positive things, and enjoying life. My new mantra–Simplifize, don't dramatize. I know "simplifize" is not a word, but it rhymes. And I would probably try to use it in Scrabble.

A drama queen is a woman who makes every issue and problem about her. Drama usually surrounds her, and if it isn't already there, she will create it. And there are plenty of drama kings out there as well! However, for the purposes of this chapter, I will stick with the drama queen terminology.

Here are some things that may indicate that you are dealing with a drama queen:

- She keeps tabs on everyone just in case she needs material to create drama
- She gives with the expectation of receiving
- She makes a big deal out of little things
- She stirs things up by gossiping and manipulating to cause trouble and arguments with others
- She never sees herself as part of the problem–there is always someone or something else to blame
- She is never satisfied unless she gets her way
- She demands compassion but extends none
- She dramatically shares the highs and lows of her life and expects

others to "ooh" and "aah" over the things she shares

- She likes being the center of attention and thrives on the chaos she creates

Drama queens aren't usually that self-aware, and you may hear them say, "I don't do drama," which makes me wonder if I am one because I am writing this chapter and saying I don't like drama!

Of course, the Bible never used the term drama queen. I think it's probably more of an urban dictionary thing. But drama queens go way back in time, and there are certainly some examples in the Bible.

Here are a few:
- Rachel, Jacob's wife, had a big rivalry with her sister Leah, also Jacob's wife. Jacob loved Rachel the most, but she was unable to conceive. On the other hand, Leah had had numerous children. Rachel said, "give me children, or I will die!" (Genesis 30:1 BSB).

- Jezebel was a jealous, vengeful queen married to King Ahab. Next to where they lived, there was a vineyard that Ahab envied and desired. The owner declined to part with the vineyard. In turn, Jezebel falsely accused him of cursing God and the king, resulting in his death. (I Kings 21:5-16)

So, what can we do to minimize the drama in our lives?

<u>Choose our friends carefully</u>

The Bible tells us, *"the righteous choose their friends carefully"* (Proverbs 12:26). I'm lucky enough to have pretty much drama-free friends at this point, and I think that's by design. I have distanced myself from friends that I've had in the past that demonstrated drama-queeny behaviors regularly. Take an inventory of your friends and focus on those who are building you up, not tearing you down or draining you emotionally and spiritually.

<u>Establish boundaries and limit time with drama-filled coworkers and family members</u>

You may have coworkers and family members who tend to be drama queens. During my career in the Human Resources field, I have encountered quite a few. They thrive on stirring things up in the workplace and often display a victim mentality. They are often what we call frequent flyers in the HR department.

I also have a few family members (one of whom I birthed) who tend to get mired in drama. It's not so easy to avoid the drama where they are involved. You can choose your friends but not your family!

When dealing with dramatic coworkers, family members, and friends, I recommend erecting some boundaries around your time and avoid engaging in their drama when you can.

Don't enable them

Enabling is ignoring the issue and allowing people to continue with their bad behavior. Jesus never enabled others to continue with sinful, unhealthy behaviors. He empowered them to change.

Pray for them

Ask Jesus to purify their hearts so that they can refresh rather than repel others. And ask him to help you with your reactions!

If you think you might be a drama queen, use this PEACE acronym to help overcome this tendency:

- **P** plan to go to God first when you feel the need for the attention and affirmation of others
- **E** endeavor to be quiet (think and pray before you speak)
- **A** avoid obsessing over your image and let God get the glory
- **C** cease from telling dramatic stories
- **E** entrust the Lord with your problems, knowing that he will address them in his perfect timing

When we know God through Jesus Christ, there is no need to engage in pointless drama!

Keep calm and be drama-free!

REFLECT

- What are some actions that you will take to reduce the drama in your life?

_____
_____
_____
_____
_____
_____
_____
_____

85

Surviving Organizational Politics

Does your workplace feel like an episode of *Survivor* where you need to determine who you'll trust, who you won't, and who you'll form alliances with? I hope not! But every organization has some degree of workplace politics, even churches and non-profits. As Aristotle said, "man is by nature a political animal."

Politics in an organization involves gaining power and influence over others to further one's own interests at the expense of others. Employees engage in politics to compete for recognition, promotions, and pay raises, or to ensure that their jobs are secure. Politicking can involve activities such as brown-nosing, withholding information, backstabbing, and stealing credit.

Author John Maxwell contrasts politics to production:
- Politicking depends upon who I know, not how I grow.
- Politicking puts focus on what I say and not on what I do.
- Politicking makes me appear better than I am rather than becoming better than I appear.
- Politicking takes shortcuts rather than provide substance.
- Politicking does what is popular rather than what is necessary.
- Politicking lets others control our destiny rather than control our own destiny.
- Politicking hopes to be given the next level, rather than grow into the next level.
- Politicking bases decisions on opinions rather than principles.

Jesus told his disciples: *"Behold, I am sending you out as sheep in the midst of wolves, so be wise as serpents and innocent as doves"* (Matthew 10:16 ESV). Jesus reminds us that we live in a fallen world, and therefore need to be on guard against the evil that may come from others. This doesn't mean that we have to cower to others or be gullible pawns. We should be wise as the serpent but, at the same time, harmless like the dove, even if it makes us seem vulnerable. We must rely on God's wisdom to stand behind our principles and to accomplish his purposes. In short, we have to find a balance between wisdom and kindness and know how to exercise the right traits at the right times.

Here are some things that you can do to survive organizational politics:
- Act with integrity. Pray and ensure that you're not acting in sin and that your attitudes are right before the Lord.
- Examine yourself first before you judge or critique another individual.
- Help in resolving conflict where appropriate.
- Control your emotions and pray when politics are at their peak. Get God's perspective on the situation and point people to Him.
- Don't listen to or engage in gossip.
- Help in any way you can, and purposefully love everyone equally.
- Don't tell untruths, and don't support or encourage sin. If you can't do this, ask the Lord about securing other employment.

As Christians, we are called to be the "*salt*" and "*light*" of the world (Matthew 5:13-15), and this includes our workplace and other organizations that we are involved with. Politics often lead to undesirable consequences such as workplace injustice, hostilities, discrimination, hurt, and stress. As salt has healing properties, we are responsible for bringing healing to our organizations by counteracting wounds caused by politics. In Old Testament times, God placed servants like Nehemiah at the right place at the right time to fulfill His purpose. In modern times, God continues to place some of us in positions to transform our organizations for the better.

REFLECT

- On a scale of 1 to 10, how would you rate your organization in terms of workplace politics?
- What will you do to be the "salt" and the "light" of your workplace?

_____
_____
_____
_____
_____
_____

86

Bypassing Bullying

We are called to love our neighbors, but some people can make it extremely difficult. Bullies are probably amongst the most difficult to love. Let's explore what bullying is. A simple definition is "one who uses superior strength or power to intimidate people." As further definition, it is harmful, targeted behavior that can happen in the workplace, at church, in the community, or in life in general. You can even be married to or in a close relationship with a bully!

I have seen bullying in action more than I'd like to admit over the years. At work, I have witnessed bullying bosses and team members. I have also seen bullying occur outside of work, even at church! It's probably most difficult to deal with situations where you have a child who is being bullied. I believe that this hurts more and is even more challenging to deal with than when you are being bullied yourself.

You would think that adults would be past bullying others, but many did not change their ways after middle and high school. They take their insecurities into their adult lives and pick on others they view as weak and susceptible. To expand on this, I don't think that people set out to bully others or cause them pain. In most cases, there is probably some underlying reason that is motivating them to act this way. This may often be a result of their own experience and pain. Maybe they were even bullied, and this is their way of dealing with that.

The Bible does not speak specifically about bullies or bullying, but many biblical principles apply to the issue:

- Love your neighbor as yourself (Mark 12:31)
- Don't intimidate or manipulate people (James 1:27, 1 John 3:17-18)
- Treat others the way we would like to be treated (Luke 6:31)
- Every person, regardless of their looks and actions, is created in the image of God (Genesis 1:26-27)

Jesus was a victim of constant bullying from His enemies. When the high priest questioned Jesus soon before he was crucified, a temple official slapped

Jesus in the face for daring to speak the truth. Jesus did not back down from these religious persecutors. He stood his ground and demanded to know why the official had lashed out.

If we are bullied, we should respond in a Christ-like manner. Here are some principles to keep in mind.

Remember who you are in Christ

The first thing we can do is remember who we are in Christ and that we are fearfully and wonderfully made. (Psalm 139) We shouldn't allow the lies bullies tell us to influence what we think of ourselves. God loves and cherishes us. We were even made in His image!

Don't seek revenge

As tempting as it may be, we shouldn't try to get back at a bully or seek revenge. As Christians, we must remember that God is the one that can judge the world in righteousness, not us. (Romans 12:17-19)

Respond with kindness and love

We should respond to the bully with kindness and love. Easier said than done, right? Scripture tells us that we should love our enemies and pray for them. (Matthew 5:44) And we should overwhelm our opponents with the goodness and love of God. (Romans 12:21) Perhaps in showing them kindness, their hearts will be softened to Christ.

Forgive

Forgiving isn't excusing their behavior or allowing them to continue in their abusiveness. Rather, it's more about your heart than theirs. Showing forgiveness will keep your heart free from bitterness, revenge, or the need for retribution.

Remember that the bully isn't your real enemy—Satan is. He will use others to take your eyes off of God's love. And remember that God can intervene in the lives of others, even bullies, to change them into the likeness of Christ for the building of God's kingdom. Remember…nothing is too hard for God!

REFLECT

* Are you dealing with a bully in your life currently? If so, how will you follow the tips shared in this lesson?

_____
_____
_____
_____

87

Being a Team Player

"Two are better than one, because they have a good return for their labor: If either of them falls down, one can help the other up. But pity anyone who falls and has no one to help them up. Also, if two lie down together, they will keep warm. But how can one keep warm alone? Though one may be overpowered, two can defend themselves. A cord of three strands is not quickly broke" (Ecclesiastes 4:9-12).

We work as part of a team in many aspects of our lives, including work, church, and community. In *The Wisdom of Teams: Creating the High-Performance Organization*, Katzenback and Smith define a team as "a small number of people with complementary skills who are committed to a common purpose, performance goals and approach for which they hold themselves mutually accountable." Teams bring together skills and experience that exceed those of any individual on the team. As the saying goes, "No one of us is as smart as all of us." Incidentally, this is why God has given each of us different spiritual gifts and talents.

I'm sure we have all been a part of teams where some members didn't demonstrate team-oriented behaviors. These individuals may have worked towards their agendas, caused rifts in the team, and impacted overall performance. One department/team I worked with had Dueling Directors fighting to see who would win control of the department. Each had their direct reports (or factions). As you can probably guess, this resulted in a dysfunctional team that was not united and working towards a common goal. The wrong team leadership filters down to the rest of the team.

The first examples of teamwork in the Bible are in Genesis, where we find the Trinity: The Father, Son, and Holy Spirit working in concert at creation (Genesis 1:1-3). Each team member had a role in creating the world and a defined job to perform. Then, God made Adam and Eve, the first human team. They were designed to complement each other and reflect the image and the community of the Trinity. (Genesis 1:26-27) Jesus assembled a twelve-man team to act as his disciples and spread the gospel. (Mark 3:13-18, Luke 6:12-16)

As Christians, it's kind of a no-brainer that we should act as team players. The

Bible strongly emphasizes that Christians must learn to work together effectively. The Scriptures reveal that members of the team that God is assembling must not be divided into factions but should *"all speak the same thing"* and *"be perfectly joined together in the same mind and in the same judgment" (1 Corinthians 1:10 NKJV).*

Here are some descriptors of how a team player should behave:

- **A team player is committed to the cause.** Instead of fostering their own agendas, team players are focused on the team and organization's goals. Philippians 2:2 (BSB) tells us to be *"likeminded, having the same love, being united in spirit and purpose."* When everyone on a team is focused on the same purpose, the team will do great things.

- **A team player is committed to resolving conflict.** Conflict is inevitable, and you need to have some productive conflict to have an effective team. The determination to resolve the conflict is the key to success. Team players should take responsibility for team unity, *"making every effort to keep the unity of the Spirit through the bond of peace" (Ephesians 4:3 CSB).* Team members who argue, disagree, and compete with each other will disrupt and hinder a team's efforts to succeed.

- **A team player encourages and supports the other team members.** Most people have no difficulty working with someone whose gifts and talents pose no threat to their standing on the team. Your character is truly proven when you can root for those who have the same gifts you have. Proverbs 3:27 (BSB) says, *"Do not withhold good from those who deserve it, when it is in your power to act."*

- **A team player tries to bring a healthy self to the team.** When you're walking with the Lord, it stands to reason that you will be a better team player. A physically, emotionally, and spiritually healthy person is more apt to be a contributing member of a team. Paul commended the church in Macedonia because *"they gave themselves first to the Lord" (2 Corinthians 8:5)* and then were able to give to others.

- **A team player doesn't care who gets the credit or the glory.** A team player is more concerned about whether the work of the team gets done than personally getting any credit. They are also apt to give credit and recognition to others for their achievements.

- **A team player can adapt and adjust.** Teams and organizations that do not anticipate and adjust to change will likely not be around for the long haul. Team players adjust to and support change for the good of the organization and the team.

- **A team player sees their role as valuable, no matter how small.** Some roles are more behind-the-scenes than others. The mature team player knows that a team cannot function without all members working together and pulling their weight.

- **A team player submits to authority.** The team player respects, supports, and points others to follow the leader. Hebrews 13:17 (BSB) says,

    Obey your leaders and submit to them, for they watch over your souls as those who must give an account. To this end, allow them to lead with joy and not with grief, for that would be of no advantage to you.

REFLECT

- Are you a good team player, or do you have opportunities to improve in this area?

- What could you do differently to be the best team member possible?

88

Victory Over Victim Mentality

We have all been victimized in our lives. Maybe bad things happened in your childhood. You had a tough breakup. You lost your job. You suffered the loss of a loved one. Bad things happen to all of us. How we respond to these things makes a big difference.

Have you ever been guilty of having a victim mentality? This involves blaming others or your circumstances for what happens in your world. An individual with a victim mentality thinks that the future only holds bad things for him or her.

The deception, "It's never my fault," is at the core of the victim mentality. My daughter has been known to say, "Things never work out for me" and "The odds are always against me." This shows a victim mentality. And for sure, she has been a victim—as we all have.

This may sound strange, but sometimes people get comfortable being the victim. They grow used to feeling sorry for themselves and inviting others to join them. They like having pity parties. I know I love a good pity party once in a while, complete with Hallmark movies and ice cream.

The Bible validates that there are certainly victims in life. *"But you, God, see the trouble of the afflicted; you consider their grief and take it in hand. The victims commit themselves to you; you are the helper of the fatherless"* (Psalm 10:14).

This verse tells us that if we commit ourselves to God, He will help us to overcome! God does not want those moments when you have been victimized to become a mindset that will affect everything that happens in your life. He wants your mindset to be that of a victor! He wants your mindset to reflect, *"I can do all things through Christ who strengthens me."*

Jesus is the ultimate example of someone who was victimized but never had a victim mentality. Can you fathom everything that he endured? They whipped him, plucked his beard, spat at him, mocked him, put a crown of thorns on his head, hung him from a cross. And he was completely blameless. Jesus never complained about how he was treated or felt sorry for himself. First Peter 2:22-23 says, *"He committed no sin, and no deceit was found in His mouth. When they hurled their insults at him, he did not retaliate; when he suffered, he made no threats. Instead, he entrusted himself to him who judges justly."*

Remember Joseph? He is another example of someone who could have easily slipped into a victim mentality. He was sold into slavery by his brothers and then falsely accused by a woman who wanted to seduce him. Later, he was forgotten by a man who promised to put in a word for him to help him get out of jail. I think I would have a chip on my shoulder after going through all of that! Check out how Joseph reacted when he encountered his brothers again:

But Joseph said to them, "Don't be afraid. Am I in the place of God? You intended to harm me, but God intended it for good to accomplish what is now being done, the saving of many lives. So then, don't be afraid. I will provide for you and your children." And he reassured them and spoke kindly to them (Genesis 51:19-21).

We all face struggles in our lives, but we can choose our attitude in the midst of them. We can wallow in self-pity, take no responsibility, and allow the victim mentality to cast blame on everyone and everything. Or we can start taking responsibility for our lives and our actions and be victors instead of victims!

Whenever you feel the urge to slip into a victim mentality, declare the following Scriptures over your life.

- *"But thanks be to God! He gives us the victory through our Lord Jesus Christ" (1 Corinthians 15:57).*

- *"No, in all these things we are more than conquerors through him who loved us" (Romans 8:37).*

- *"I have told you these things, so that in me you may have peace. In this world you will have trouble. But take heart! I have overcome the world" (John 16:33).*

REFLECT

- Do you ever tend to slip into a victim mentality?

- If so, what will you do to be victorious over victim mentality?

_____
_____
_____
_____
_____
_____
_____
_____

89
Don't Be a "Church Lady"

"And I tell you, you are Peter, and on this rock I will build my church, and the gates of hell shall not prevail against it" (Matthew 16:18 ESV).

Going to church is an important part of being a Christian. God wants us to have fellowship with other believers as this is a critical aspect of our faith. However, some people make it difficult for others to feel welcomed and unencumbered in the church.

Who remembers the Church Lady from Saturday Night Live? She was an older woman named "Enid Strict," played by Dana Carvey, who was the uptight, smug, judgmental, and pious host of a talk show called Church Chat. She was a spoof of "holier-than-thou" churchgoers. The interview with her "guests" would start okay and eventually degrade into a tirade against their lack of piety and secular lifestyles. She was known for phrases like, "Well, isn't that *SPE-CIAL*?!", "*How con-VEEN-ient!*", and "Could it be...*SATAN*?"

Dana Carvey said this character was inspired by some of the women in the church where he grew up who were judgmental and always kept track of attendance. Do you know or have you known any "Church Ladies?" I certainly have. Some of them are alive and well in our churches today, and their attitudes and behaviors can make people feel "less than" and drive them away. And they aren't always ladies. There are some "Church Gentlemen" as well.

Everything I'm hearing indicates that church attendance is declining for the younger generations. I think that some of this is based on the perceived expectation that you must act a certain way and dress a certain way to be accepted as part of the church. I am not insinuating that exclusive, judgmental behavior happens in all church environments, but it does still happen. I am involved in several church committees and have witnessed folks that are constantly critical and judgmental of what is going on at church. This can include being prideful about their involvement in the church, criticizing others for behaviors and appearance that don't fit in with their beliefs, and looking down on and talking about others in the church based on what they are or aren't doing.

I don't believe that there is a place in the church for folks like the Church Lady (unless they change their behavior). They make people feel bad and drive them away. Over the years, I have visited a few churches that were not friendly or inclusive and seemed to look down on those that weren't like them. My friends have a bi-racial child, and they felt shunned when they visited a local church. I have heard the same from others that felt rejected due to their sexual orientation. I'd like to think of the church as the most inclusive environment there is, but this isn't the case in a lot of situations. Largely due to folks like the Church Lady.

Psalm 96:3-4 (ESV) says, *"Declare his glory among the nations, his marvelous works among all the peoples! For great is the Lord, and greatly to be praised; he is to be feared above all gods."* Notice that this is inclusive and says, *"all the peoples,"* not just those that fit into a certain mold and attend church every Sunday.

So, what's the point of this chapter? If you are a Church Lady, quit acting "holier-than-thou" and welcome others into the church! After all, we are all sinners, and we all have issues that we need to work through. If you are attending or a member of a church where you encounter a Church Lady, try to get past this behavior and find a group that you connect with. The church is made up of humans, so it will never be perfect. However, the encouragement and support of a church family are very important on our journey to learn and grow as Christians.

REFLECT

- If you are involved in a church, how can you help ensure that people aren't driven away by "Church Ladies or Gentlemen?"

- If you are not involved in a church, consider checking some out or getting involved in a Bible Study group. It's important and will help you to grow in your faith!

Issues, Issues, and More Issues

I sure seem to have a lot of issues, but I guess I am a self-proclaimed "hot mess." To be fair, not every chapter in this book deals with my issues, but many of them do. I started my book with thirty days of messages, which grew to sixty and ended with ninety. I am pretty confident that most of us have our fair share of issues, even if we don't admit it to ourselves or others.

As I mentioned early in the book, I have felt called to share my struggles and imperfections. Lucky me! I always enjoyed writing in a work or school capacity but never thought of taking it beyond that. However, I kept feeling this tug on my heart that God wanted me to write. I started by reading a lot of Christian non-fiction books and journaling. Then, I decided to start a blog, knowing that I may turn some people off in the process (which is hard for a recovering people-pleaser). Anyhow, I started and never stopped, and it's been all God.

We talked about the concept of calling early in this book. But I thought we might explore it in more detail because that is truly what led me to write this book. A calling is a tug on our hearts toward a particular thing that comes from God. It can be for a specific situation, a season of life, or our lifetime. God calls each of us to different things, such as relationships, jobs, ministries, locations, etc., at different times in our lives. He even calls "hot messes" to minister to others.

If we feel that tug on our hearts, how do we know if it's from God or our desires?

The calling will be consistent with Scripture

God's callings for us will always draw us closer to Him and be consistent with Scripture. *"All Scripture is God-breathed and is useful for teaching, rebuking, correcting and training in righteousness, so that the servant of God may be thoroughly equipped for every good work"* (2 Timothy 3:16-17).

You will feel at peace

Although you may be afraid at first, if the calling is from God, you will feel God's overwhelming peace to do what he is asking. *"And the peace of God,* which transcends all understanding, will guard your hearts and your minds in Christ Jesus" (Philippians 4:7).

You will get what you need to fulfill this calling.

He will never call us to something without also equipping us to do what He's asking us to do.

You will receive confirmation.

God will likely confirm what He's asking you to do through situations and/or other people.

I have the continued feeling that He wants me to write, so I will stay the course and continue my blog and work on another book. Thankfully, I don't think I have enough material for a *Confessions of a Hot Mess Two*.

> "'For I know that plans I have for you,' declares the Lord, 'plans to prosper you and not to harm you, plans to give you hope and a future'" (Jeremiah 29:11).

REFLECT

- Have you ever felt called to do something? If so, what was it?
- What do you feel God is calling you to do now? If you aren't sure, pray for guidance.

Leslie Speas

Section 7:

Bonus Chapters

Dear Younger Me

I'm not sure how it happened, but I am now in my fifties! Somehow, I thought it would take a lot longer to get to this age! Some things are not so great about getting older–gray hair, hot flashes, chin hair, wrinkles, gravity… I'll stop there as I'm getting depressed. But there are some positive things about being in this stage of life. Here are a few:

- I have time to read and take naps.
- I don't have to worry about feeding other people (not that I was ever very good at that)–my husband usually fends for himself.
- I care less about accumulating stuff and more about keeping things simple.
- I care less about what people think of me.
- I have time to volunteer more and get involved in the community.
- I don't operate a "taxi service" any longer–probably showing my age mentioning taxis!
- I'm better at managing my emotions.

Here are some things that I would tell "younger me" if I could go back in time:

- Accept and love yourself as God made you. Quit comparing yourself to others and understand that God made you the way you are for a reason–he doesn't make mistakes. Get counseling if you need to work through your issues. You must love yourself before you can love and nurture others.
- Don't worry so much about what other people think. You are never going to please everyone. You need to be true to yourself and set boundaries. Also, don't waste your time on mean people that don't treat you with respect.
- Children are a blessing and a joy, but if you have them, keep in mind that they will break your heart and scare you to death more

times than you could ever imagine. And you aren't done when they are in their twenties and beyond, as I thought would be the case. Puppies are a good lower maintenance substitute. Just sayin'.

- Tips on raising kids

    - Chill out on the activities—they probably aren't going to be soccer stars or ballerinas. Doing so much running wears them out and wears you out too.

    - Let your kids fail—I always tried to protect my kids from failure and disappointment and would jump in to help wherever I could. I am embarrassed to admit it, but I even did all of my older daughter's college applications for her. Life is filled with difficult times and failures, and our children need to learn to deal with them effectively, even though it is hurtful and difficult for us to watch.

    - Make your kids help with the housework!

    - Quit feeling guilty about time away from your kids if you work outside the home or have other obligations. This isn't productive. Just focus on the quality of the time you have!

- Don't sweat the small stuff and spend so much time worrying about things that will not matter in the future. Is it going to matter after even a day if your kid insisted on wearing an outfit that didn't match? Or you got a snarky email from someone at work?

- Slow down! Being busy is not a badge of honor. Set boundaries and stick to them. Figure out what's important to you and say no to things that don't fit these criteria.

- Make time to be still. If you give yourself ten to fifteen minutes of quiet time in the morning, you'll start your day from a centered, calm state so that no matter what happens, you'll be able to respond thoughtfully rather than react instinctively.

- You probably can't have it all. Focus more on relationships and less on building bank balances and climbing the career ladder. In the end, relationships are what will matter, especially your relationship with God.

- Exercise and eat right. Yay! There is one that I did consistently. As a result, I haven't had struggles with my weight or health problems. I also think I may have gone off the deep end if I didn't exercise because it helps me manage stress. I can even still do plyometrics (jump training), only sometimes I pee.

- Choose a partner wisely and well. Don't go for the bad boys—you won't be able to change them; only God can do that. And it isn't your partner's job to fill the emptiness inside you. That's God too. Be with someone who will treat you well and takes care of your soul. And don't settle, even if you feel it's time that you find a partner. It's better to be single than in a difficult, unfulfilling relationship.

P.S. Also, stay out of the sun and try not to squint.

Hope this helps someone! The end.

Bonus Reflection: What advice would you give your younger self?

BONUS
Why Can't People Be More Like Dogs?

Dogs are awesome. God made dogs for us as companions and helpers—and to give us pleasure and happiness. Dogs can also provide us with some lessons on how to better Christians. And DOG is also GOD spelled backward. Maybe there's a reason for that...

Dogs provide companionship and loyalty. They love you unconditionally and don't expect you to do much in return besides feeding and walking them. And mine expect treats a lot, but that's my fault. Funny story that doesn't have much to do with this. I had my dog in training classes, and she and I did not do so well. We ended up in "time out." And the instructor made me play like I was the dog as I guess I wasn't getting it. We never did graduate.

Below are some things that we can learn from dogs:

Love unconditionally

They don't care about our status, where we live, what car we drive, who we know, or if we are having a bad hair day. Trust me, my dogs have seen me looking very frightening and don't seem to mind. They are never ashamed of us or worried if we will fit in with their dog friends. Do you know how sometimes you can feel the "mean" and "judgment" in people? You don't get that from dogs. They will always be by your side. They only care that you are there!

In our world, we often treat people differently if they don't come with a certain status or they act in ways that we think they should. Dogs provide a great example of how we should love other people.

> *Love is patient, love is kind. It does not envy, it does not boast, it is not proud. It does not dishonor others, it is not self-seeking, it is not easily angered, it keeps no record of wrongs. Love does not delight in evil but rejoices with the truth. It always protects, always trusts, always hopes, always perseveres (1 Corinthians 13:4-7).*

Live in the moment

Dogs don't have a big master plan or think about yesterday or tomorrow.

They simply live in the moment. They take the time to smell the roses and stick their heads out the window. They are not preoccupied with what was or will be. They eat, play, and rest when they want or need to. *"Therefore do not worry about tomorrow, for tomorrow will worry about itself. Each day has enough trouble of its own"* (Matthew 6:34).

Don't hold grudges

If you refuse your dog a treat, he doesn't stay mad at you. Or hold a grudge for even a minute. When we retain a grudge, we give someone we don't like power over our emotions, which only hurts us. *"Do not seek revenge or bear a grudge against anyone among your people, but love your neighbor as yourself. I am the Lord"* (Leviticus 19:18).

Play!

Dogs take time to play and move their bodies. Exercise and play are good for the soul and body. We should do more of the same! It would surely bring more joy and happiness to our lives. *"And the streets of the city shall be full of boys and girls playing in its streets"* (Zechariah 8:5).

Show compassion

Who is the first to comfort you when you are crying or feeling upset? For me, it's usually the dogs. It's like they know when you need comfort or a snuggle. We don't know what another person has gone through—or is going through. We should act like dogs, meet them where they are, and show them some compassion. Everyone is going through something, be like a dog, and be there for them. *"Be kind and compassionate to one another, forgiving each other, just as in Christ God forgave you"* (Ephesians 4:32).

Accept and love yourself

Do dogs think, "I wish I was tall and thin like that Great Dane" or "I wish my nose looked like a pug?" I guess we don't know for sure, but I'm pretty confident that dogs don't care what others think about them. They come in all shapes and sizes as we do. I don't think they spend time comparing themselves or wishing they were something that they aren't. You were made as you are for a purpose. Embrace yourself as you are, as dogs do! *"For you formed my inward parts; you knitted me together in my mother's womb. I praise you, for I am fearfully and wonderfully made"* (Psalm 139:13-14).

Be loyal

Loyalty is essential for building and maintaining strong relationships. We could learn a lesson from dogs in how we show loyalty to our friends and loved ones. Your dog's loyalty will always be there, even if you feel you have lost everything else. *"Don't urge me to leave you or to turn back from you. Where you go I will go, and where you stay I will stay. Your people will be my people and your God my God"* (Ruth 1:16).

<u>Greet others enthusiastically</u>

How great does it feel when you come home and your dog is wagging his/her tail and acting happy to see you? We should greet our friends, loved ones, and even coworkers enthusiastically and let them know we are glad to see them. Maybe don't wag your tail, though. *"All the brothers send you greetings. Greet one another with a holy kiss"* (1 Corinthians 16:20 ESV).

As you can see, there is a lot we can learn about how to treat others (and ourselves) from dogs. I know my pups bring lots of joy to my life. Although sometimes they are productivity killers when they are napping or snuggled up, and I feel it necessary to join in.

It's extremely hard to lose a pet as they are part of the family—and we sometimes like them better than other family members. However, I truly believe that I will see them again in heaven. I have read some different opinions about whether dogs go to heaven, but I choose to believe they do. I told my daughter that one of my visions of heaven involved sitting on a soft cloud with lots of pillows, coffee, and chocolate with soft fuzzy dogs all around—but they don't poop, pee, or bark in heaven.

The next chapter is what we can learn from cats. Just kidding—I like cats but not quite the same situation if you've ever read the thing where it talks about the mind of a dog and a cat.

Bonus Reflection: If you don't have a dog, think about getting one. They are awesome! Do you have any other thoughts on what we can learn from dogs?

In Conclusion

I hope that the lessons in this book have been helpful. It has been rather cathartic for me. I've learned more about myself, and I have also learned a lot about God. There seem to be some definite themes that have emerged in the various chapters, such as:

- Work on getting to know yourself better. This will help you to understand what you are called to do! Identify and try to overcome any negative narratives that may be driving you.

- Take care of yourself. Spend time doing activities that are good for your soul, including rest!

- Spend time with God. Try to spend some quiet time with God each day in whatever way works best for you—reading the Bible or a devotional, walking in nature, and praying are all examples.

- Think about what you think about. If it's not in line with God's Word, try to redirect your thoughts.

- Find ways to serve and help others. Doing this will undoubtedly enrich your life.

- Be grateful for the people and things that you have in your life. Try to focus on what you DO have, instead of what you don't.

- Let go and let God. We aren't in control, so why try to be? Cast your cares on the Lord!

Thanks for going on this journey with me! I hope it has helped you and that some of the chapters speak to issues you are facing.

REFLECT

- Which of these "themes" do you need to work on?
- What will you do to progress in these areas?

Sources

Introduction
Chip Ingram, *Holy Ambition: Turning God-Shaped Dreams into Reality* (Brentwood, Tennessee: Living on the Edge, 2017).

Four
Rick Warren D. Min, Daniel Amen M.D. Mark Hyman M.D., *The Daniel Plan: 40 Days to a Healthier Life* (Grand Rapids, Michigan: Zondervan, 2013).

Eight
Beverly Engel, *The Emotionally Abusive Relationship: How to Stop Being Abused and How to Stop Abusing* (Hoboken, New Jersey: John Wiley & Sons, 2002).

Ten, Thirty, Forty-Four
Rick Warren, *The Purpose Driven Life: What On Earth Am I Here For?*, (Grand Rapids, Michigan: Zondervan, 2002).

Twenty-Eight
Sharon Jaynes, *Enough: Silencing the Lies That Steal Your Confidence* (Eugene, Oregon: Harvest House Publishers, 2018).

Thirty-Five
Max Lucado, *Anxious for Nothing: Finding Calm in a Chaotic World* (Nashville, Tennessee: Thomas Nelson, Inc., 2019).

Forty
Sarah Young, *Jesus Calling* (Nashville, Tennessee: Thomas Nelson, Inc., 2004).

Forty-Five
Charismamag.com/life/women/9790are-you-a-people-pleaser-instead-of-a-god-pleaser.

Lysa TerKeurst, *The Best Yes: Making Wise Decisions in the Midst of Endless Demands* (Nashville, Tennessee: Thomas Nelson, Inc., 2014).

Forty-Six
Brenee Brown, *The Gifts of Imperfection: Let Go of Who You Think You're Supposed to Be and Embrace Who You Are* (New York, New York: Simon & Schuster, 2010).

Forty-Seven
Sharon Hodde Miller, *Free of Me: Why Life is Better When It's Not About You* (Ada, Michigan: Baker Books, 2017).

Fifty-Three
Joyce Meyer, *The Power of a Simple Prayer: How to Talk With God About Everything* (Nashville, Tennessee: Faithwords, 2007).

Sixty-Five
LysaTerKeurst, *Uninvited: Living Loved When You Feel Less Than, Left Out and Lonely* (Nashville, Tennessee: Thomas Nelson, Inc., 2016).

Seventy
LysaTerKeurst, *It's Not Supposed to Be This Way: Finding Unexpected Strength When Disappointments Leave You Shattered* (Nashville, Tennessee: Thomas Nelson, Inc., 2018).

Eighty
Elisa Pulliam, *Unblinded Faith: Gaining Spiritual Sight Through Believing God's Word* (Eugene, Oregon: Harvest House Publishers, 2018).

Eighty-Seven
Jon R. Katzenback and Douglas K. Smith, *The Wisdom of Teams: Creating the High-Performance Organization* (Brighton, Massachusetts: Harvard Business Review Press, 2015).

Scripture is from the NIV Bible unless otherwise noted.

THE HOLY BIBLE, NEW INTERNATIONAL VERSION®, NIV® Copyright © 1973, 1978, 1984, 2011 by Biblica, Inc.